THE
TEXTILE
TOUCH

How Five-Star Hospitality and Heritage
Brands Create Their Signature Style
Through Textiles

KATIE YOUNG GERALD

RƎTHINK PRESS

First published in Great Britain 2018
by Rethink Press (www.rethinkpress.com)

© Copyright Katie Young Gerald

Cover image © Jim Spelman
www.jimspelmanvisuals.com

Praise

"Katie Young is a talented, committed and knowledgeable designer. Combining her experience at my UK-based luxury fashion house with her 20 years of sourcing in Asia and her focus on business branding, she knows exactly how to enhance your brand with her company Bespoke Textiles. In this book she explains how she designs, streamlines a homogenous image, and sources sustainably for the luxury hospitality and heritage industry."

Helen David, Founder
English Eccentrics

'Katie has eloquently put together a clear model that reflects her business journey. She gives a fascinating insight in to the textiles industry and how she has incorporated this with the world of hospitality.'

Monica Or, Hospitality Consultant
Star Quality Hospitality Consultancy

'What could be a daunting task is broken down in such a way that whether this is the first time you have been involved in this process or you are a veteran, the end result will enable you to clearly define your brand with style that is not only simple but elegant.'

Michael Berg, Group Creative Director
The Hospital Club London and Los Angeles

Contents

Foreword

Here is Katie Young Gerald's first book, *The Textile Touch*, which brings together within its pages not only years of experience, but also the knowledge that has been used to help brands create a signature style through their relationship with textiles.

I am deeply honoured to have been asked to write this foreword for a remarkable member of one of the largest of the United Kingdom's successful creative industries. When I met Katie for the first time, I was struck by the simple joy and passion she brought to her work. Her enthusiasm is contagious, and it has certainly led to her being at the pinnacle of her career: an expert in working with hospitality companies and developing with them both the tangible and intangible characteristics that identify a brand.

Katie's work is bold, original and distinctive, yet it never draws attention away from the brand; it merely enhances and reinforces it. Elegance and simplicity epitomise her work, which reflects a relaxed, urbane lifestyle. Not only does her approach have a positive impact on the look of the brand, but also on how customers interact with, and relate to, the brand.

The book details Katie's love of style and textiles, and how this has shaped so many of the brands that we interact with on an almost daily basis – there is no doubt that she has made a significant impact. In simple steps Katie takes us through the process that all hospitality and heritage brands need to go through if they wish to refresh or reju-venate their brand, with a focus on their uniforms. What could be a daunting task is broken down in such a way that whether this is the first time you have been involved in this process or you are a veteran of it, Katie's approach will enable you to define your brand clearly with a style that not only looks good but expresses your values.

From the start of her career with the great Betty Jackson to the early days of English Eccentrics, it has been an extraordinary journey. Join Katie on this journey and learn the secrets of a career spanning twenty-five years. Her experience, skills and genuine enthusiasm for her work illustrate how much importance a brand should place on uniforms and on their relationship with textiles

in general. By embracing Katie's perspective and methodology, you will be able to create a solid foundation for a
truly successful and sustainable brand.

Michael Berg
Group Creative Director, the Hospital Club,
London and Los Angeles

Introduction

People often think style is something you either have or don't have; that only creative people or people with lots of money can be truly stylish. Even then, it's hit or miss. Let me assure you that this is not the case. Style is something everyone can have.

If you really know your style and how to express it, you can be very astute with little money. And if you can manage this at a personal level, why can't companies with greater resources and a vital business image to project do better at expressing their style? It really annoys me when hotels or restaurants don't understand that the quality and style of their textiles and uniforms are top priorities for their brand's look and feel.

Throughout this book, I will share with you the secrets of creating an outstanding, timeless style and a tailored supply chain for your staff's uniforms, textiles and more, enabling you to identify products that truly capture and communicate the unique brand essence of your business. To illustrate the insights I will be sharing, I will include examples of how they can boost your pride and your profits.

Where do you start? Who do you trust? These are questions I get asked all the time. I want to encourage you to trust your instincts when adding your own 'textiles touch' to your brand, and I will give you plenty of practical advice on dealing with suppliers. This book will give you the knowledge and hopefully the inspiration to start being bolder with your brand's style.

Using my processes, you can develop your brand further through textiles, helping you switch from dull, impractically low-end off-the-shelf workwear and interiors to style and quality that will reflect your brand's unique identity. It may be possible to improve on what you already have, as long as it is right for you, your customer, your brand and your team, or you may need to start again. Either way, I am confident that this book will give you the skills and knowledge you require to make your brand stand out through its style.

Whether you are a dabbling designer, or you are in the process of becoming a huge brand or hotel group, there will be something in this book that will be of value to you and will help you move forward with an aspect of your business you may currently be stuck on. Through my numerous case studies and stories, I will show you how to make progress at every stage with relative ease, from fitting to funding, fabrics to fashion, delivery to deadlines.

But first, let me take you through my journey into style.

CHAPTER ONE

A Passion
For Style

My home town of Burnham-on-Sea, Somerset, is a Victorian seaside town that many people retire to. When the residents pass away or have clear-outs, their possessions are donated to a number of charity/antique shops dotted around the town. For some reason, though, when I lived there, most residents of Burnham-on-Sea wouldn't have been seen dead in these wonderful little shops. Nobody used them, with the exception of a few elderly ladies – and me. I loved them because they contained fantastic clothes. Going through the door of the charity shops, I would feel as if I was stepping back in time, surrounded by unique clothes and accessories. I loved the excitement of discovering exquisitely made items of timeless quality, both on the inside and the outside, and admiring the skill in the way the cloth had been cut. Many of the garments had fabulous embellishments, such as beading, and were made from rare and interesting fabrics.

Even the woven labels in the back of the garments – 'Made in England' or 'British made' – fascinated me.

1.1 – Use the Zappar app to scan the code and watch the video showing how to find the gold in charity shops.
https://youtu.be/LmTTvfMOL8g

Going to these shops was my favourite treat, and what started as a hobby of collecting, adjusting or altering garments soon led to me owning quite a big archive of vintage clothing. Exciting ideas began to fill my head about how I could customise an item of clothing I had found for myself or use its design to create something new.

DABBLING IN DESIGN

When I was eleven, my mum finally gave in to my pleas and bought me my very own Husqvarna sewing machine, which lasted until I was thirty-five. I was really happy, making and mending garments – so much so that I probably made thousands of items on that machine. I would spend hour upon hour altering and customising things, wearing my combination of homemade and shop-bought creations paired with something special that I had found in a charity shop. I never bought anything unless it was original and really flattered me. From my point of view, the best thing about old-fashioned clothes was that they had small body lengths with short backs, which fitted me perfectly.

> Tip : When you get your back length right, clothes never ruck up at the back.

When I was nine, I used to make my Sindy doll new clothes. 'Oh, wouldn't it be nice if Sindy could have a polo neck jumper in that lovely green, just like me?' I would think.

When I adjusted something of my own, I'd always make sure I had a little scrap of fabric left over so that I could make a garment for Sindy too. I made so many miniature clothes by hand that I eventually set up a shop on our living room fireplace, putting an advert in the local paper, the *Scan*, to sell the Sindy doll clothes for 10p each. People would happily come and buy them, even if my mum did hide whenever the doorbell rang.

Eventually, people started wanting more. They were requesting that I make them outfits similar to the ones I was putting together and wearing myself, so with a little help, I started to create patterns.

When I was twelve, my mum got a job waitressing in the evenings, and I was introduced to my babysitter, Liz. Liz was doing a foundation fashion design course at the local art college in Taunton, and she would bring sketch pads with her when she came to look after me. I loved studying her sketches. She showed me how to make template body shapes, and then add a new neckline or skirt line to each one, producing design after design until she got something she loved. When my mum remarried, Liz designed her wedding outfit. As I watched the journey an item of clothing would take, from being designed and selected to being fitted, I knew exactly what career I wanted. There was no doubt about it – I had discovered my passion for style.

My dad's wedding five months later galvanised me into looking for unique ways to dress and buy clothes. Visiting our nearest larger town, Weston-super-Mare, I was deeply unsatisfied with what was in the shops. It was poor quality, and completely unsuitable for a wedding. Eventually, I bought a pair of pink pedal pushers and a pink fluffy jumper. It wasn't going to be a traditional wedding, so I could afford to be a little bit more casual than I would have been otherwise and choose something I could wear again.

1.2 – Use the Zappar app to scan the code and watch the video showing how to fit a jacket.
www.thewardrobecurator.co.uk
https://www.youtube.com/watch?v=jsei_7dTVlw

MY NANS' INFLUENCE

Once I had been spurred on to pursue a career in fashion by my happy evenings designing clothes with Liz and my disgust at the lack of choice in the clothes shops of Weston-super-Mare, I made it clear that I wanted to dress uniquely and stylishly. Both my nans influenced me hugely, although for different reasons.

1.3 - My Mum and Step-Dad's Wedding when I was 12.

Nan from the farm was a home maker; a 'make do and mender'. She knitted, sewed, baked, and cared for everyone, even cleaning all the church brasses, and cutting and arranging flowers in the church every week. She taught me so much about recreating things from old fabrics and never wasting anything – it was she who encouraged me to make my dolls' clothes. Nan also tried to teach me to knit, but being a left-hander, I couldn't pick it up from her right-handed technique. Ironically, my nan had actually been born left-handed, too, but had been forced to learn to write with her right hand. Apparently, people once believed that being left-handed was somehow wrong. Poor thing – I can't help thinking how creative and skilled my nan was with her unnatural hand, and wondering how much better she would have been had she been allowed to develop her skills naturally.

My other nan had originally come from Essex so had grown up with much more of an influence from London. She lived for singing, socialising, dancing, and her holidays in Majorca. With a great eye for style, she was never without her scarves, colour-coordinated outfits, beautiful jewellery, flawlessly applied makeup and hair all set. Whenever I visited her, she liked me to pin-tuck her wide-leg trousers so she had a permanent crease down the centre front. Nan used to work in the local Sue Ryder charity shop, and I always made sure I popped in for a browse whenever I could.

SCHOOL, COLLEGE AND UNIVERSITY

My ultimate ambition was to work in costume for the BBC, so at school, among my ten GCSE subjects, I chose Fashion and Needlework along with Art, English and Economics. Eventually, I was accepted on the Fashion BTEC foundation course at the Somerset College of Arts in Taunton, which was where my babysitter Liz had studied.

1.4 – Use the Zappar app to scan the code and watch the video of me going through my Nan's sewing box.
https://youtu.be/xzE15_owht8

Following on from my childhood passion, one of my favourite pastimes throughout my time at art college, and then university too, was to customise and create new designs from old clothes. I learned how clothes were made by hand and that they were as interesting and beautiful on the inside as on the outside. Basically, I learned about quality fashion garment manufacturing from taking the best of the best apart.

Once I had completed my course at the Somerset College of Arts, I was accepted into my first choice university, the Manchester School of Art (then the Manchester Metropolitan University), to take a Bachelor of Arts degree in Fashion and Textiles (chiefly studying fashion). I found myself doing a highly technical and creative degree in a vibrant city. At that time, the music culture of house, garage, rave music and hippy Happy Mondays had just exploded on to the Manchester scene and was having a huge influence on fashion and clubbing, particularly when the famous Hacienda nightclub opened, and people from the whole country flocked to try and get in. Also, on the fashion side of things, there was an incredibly cool place called Afflecks Palace, which stocked the most amazing vintage clothes and pieces from really unique up-and-coming designers, much on a par with Hyper Hyper in London but a bit edgier, and quirkier, with more of a 'clubby' influence, as it was Manchester.

I took my degree seriously as I was the kind of student who works their socks off. I didn't just study hard for the end-of-year exams and play the rest of the time; I was committed to doing well right from the start, putting a massive amount of time and effort in because I really loved what I was doing. The presentations, projects and intense coursework, along with the fun new friends I made at university, were all part of me evolving as a fashion designer, a professional and eventually a serial entrepreneur.

1.5 – My graduation with my parents at Manchester Metropolitan University, receiving a BA Hons in Fashion & Textiles.

I was lucky enough to have done commission work and alterations for private clients back home, which I realised many other people on the same course hadn't done. Often, they couldn't even make clothes for themselves, so I had a practical edge. Even if I hadn't, though, my desire to do well would have kept me from standing still. Building real projects alongside studying is the only way to benefit from the learning, even if you are just experimenting on yourself.

My big break came in my final year at university when I got two weeks' work experience at Betty Jackson, an English fashion design company based in London. As part of a small team working in production, I made my first fashion friend, John. John helped me by drawing maps of where all the deliveries had to go, then I would have to pack and drive the van to Knightsbridge from Tottenham Court Road. It was terrifying driving across the centre of London, having only ever driven and navigated in Somerset before. The gears on the van had slipped, too, so I could only put it in second gear. I'm sure you can imagine how many drivers were beeping their horns at me due to my slow driving.

Despite the dodgy gearbox on the van, I left Betty Jackson with a reference which was good enough to secure me my first job.

ENGLISH ECCENTRICS

After graduating, I moved to London so that I would give myself the best possible chance of finding a job. I decided on fifty companies that I wanted to work with, from high-end luxury brands to high-street designers, and sent off job applications to them all. Despite realising that I was going to be more suited to niche, luxury clothing brands rather than fast fashion, I knew that I needed work experience.

I got my first job in 1993, the August after I had graduated, with a company called English Eccentrics, a small British textile brand based off Old Street, London. At that time, Old Street and the East End were pretty run-down areas. It was certainly not the vibrant, trendy place it is today with the likes of Nobu Hotel, Ace Hotel and Shoreditch House having their flagship sites based there. Back in 1993, only a handful of people walked out of Old Street Tube station each morning. There was nothing around apart from a few old shoe wholesalers, a sex shop, a dodgy club and the Bricklayers Arms pub. Round the corner from Charlotte Road where the studio was located, was Goodie Food, a sandwich shop, and Farmers Fastening was handy for buttons, but apart from that, it was a very depressed area.

The English Eccentrics studio was a rickety three storey building. My job was dealing with the stock arriving in the basement from the outworkers, factories, mills and suppliers, checking the fabrics and garments into stock, quality controlling and storing everything, and then allocating new stock to orders for dispatching or materials to dockets. I worked with the fabulous Karen. Karen introduced me to the grand art of list making, which has now become one of my biggest daily joys. I make more lists than I have hot dinners – they really help me focus my mind and get things done.

1.6/1.7 – Working for English Eccentrics – Royal Visit from Princess Anne where I'm explaining the process of checking the silk velvet, to making the lay plans for placement print of pattern pieces on a panel.

Karen taught me how to organise the elements of a professional fashion company from the bottom up. This helped me to understand all the ordering processes, from the haberdashery to the fabrics. I loved getting to know everything that was involved in the running of a fashion brand, and especially enjoyed meeting all the suppliers as they delivered the garments. As I was the one who inspected every single garment and panel of fabric, if there were any errors, I would also be the one to bring up the issues with the manufacturers or outworkers.

There were several suppliers I'll never forget. Ralph, a retired factory owner, fed work to talented homeworkers all over London. He would go around delivering samples and orders to his band of workers, and then collecting the samples and garments. Ralph was an outgoing and humorous man who enjoyed connecting with others through his network, which is just how I feel today. I love the banter, the wonderful people and talents that I get to engage with while orchestrating the creation of beautifully finished products.

A group of lovely Chinese ladies came with Ralph in his tiny little van. Ralph made all the tunics and shirts himself, while Eva, an elegant Polish lady who was quite a character, made the skirts and palazzo pants, and eventually dresses too.

English Eccentrics' other key producers included Narrinder of Serenade Fashions. He was based in Leicestershire and timed his deliveries for a Friday afternoon so he could combine them with an evening out in London. The pattern grader, Malcolm, came from Southend and seemed to enjoy his day out. He was happy to stop and have a cup of tea and a chat – I think he had taken a bit of a 'shine' to me. Mrs Giglio was based in Brixton and ran an army of Italian ladies who were experts at hand rolling the hems of scarves. I occasionally paid her a visit to pick up on any quality issues, which always involved having several espressos and panettone in her living room.

STARTING A UNIQUE STYLE TREND

English Eccentrics caused devoré velvet (velvet pile burnt away in places to reveal the sheer silk chiffon underneath) to have a huge comeback in 1992/93, just at the time I joined. The company also made square printed silk scarves, creating a trend that would go global. I remember how exciting it was to meet the celebrities who would come to the studio to hand pick their own devoré velvet tunics. There were only three colour choices: navy, maroon and black, which made the tunics all the more desirable.

Witnessing this craze, I knew I wanted one, and I made sure to reserve my favourite tunic before a celebrity could beat me to it. I still have and treasure that tunic to this day.

> Tip : The key to starting a trend is to create something bespoke and unique, which makes the product all the more desirable to influencers.

When the media picked up on the amount of celebrity wearers of the devoré velvet tunics, it caused a revolution in fashion. Before long, other brands (from high-street through to designer brands) started mass producing devoré velvet products, but English Eccentrics had been the first.

1.8 – English Eccentrics Devoré Velvet 'Cameo' tunic as worn by Helena Bonham Carter.

The factory owners and suppliers who worked with English Eccentrics over the years were often well connected in the fashion industry and made stunning garments for many other designers in London. It was fascinating to check the full grade of clothing sizes and see how all the patterns looked layered on top of each other. I learned so much from being a key part of quality control, which paved the way for me to develop my skills of designing stylish clothes and accessories for the future, and also allowed me to build key relationships without which I would never have been able to bring creative projects to fruition.

SUMMARY

It takes an army of skilled practitioners to create even the day-to-day clothing we take for granted: designers, pattern cutters, finishers, fabric weavers, dyers, machine specialists, to name but a few. Add to this the administrative and production side of the garment business, and you will understand how much there was for me to learn as I started out.

Now that I have given you a glimpse of the desire and influences that led me to where I am today, it is time for me to start sharing the knowledge I've gained over the years with you. In the next chapter, I am going to take you through the basics of making your hospitality and/or heritage brand popular through your unique style and textile touches.

CHAPTER TWO

Design and
Supply

Branding and brand identity play a massive role in your business. Therefore it is important that you incorporate a tastefully designed uniform into your brand using textiles and a style your staff will look and feel great in. Your uniform needs to portray your brand's identity in a way that other people – customers, prospects, competitors and employees – will admire.

Take Virgin Atlantic, for example. Virgin's airline staff are stylish, confident and proud in their 'on-brand' designer red outfits. Richard Branson had the clever idea of commissioning Vivienne Westwood to design Virgin's uniform, making sure it was as environmentally friendly as possible by investing in a recycled polyester and wool fabric. (Read more at http://www.bespoketextiles.co.uk/blog/british-icon-dame-vivienne-westwood5865451)

You want to wow your audience in a similar way to companies like Virgin. Get inspired by classic design with a bespoke twist. If your staff love what they wear when they come to work, they will feel good. They are your brand ambassadors, so make sure you're doing them proud. Without a doubt, a well-designed and classy uniform adds the X factor to your brand. That's when you know you have found a winning combination of textile touches and timeless designs. This doesn't have to just be on your people but in your environment, your sofas, your chairs... interior designers and architects understand the importance of great looking surroundings, to make them feel good and have a quality lasting look that makes you want to hang out there forever.

If your staff are your ambassadors, your customers are your fans, so make sure your brand looks its best in every interaction you have with them – in person, in store, on site, on your website, and in your products. Not only will this give you a competitive edge, but it will also give your brand values consistency over multiple media. Isn't this the desire of every business owner who wants to build a brand that will last a lifetime and beyond?

From the point of view of your clients, a stylish uniform can increase their sense of belonging, trust and quality. These values make all the difference, effortlessly emphasising your brand, and they are becoming more and more sought-after.

A bespoke and beautifully branded label is a powerful way to add value and consistency to your products, and to your brand. You can extend its use across a range of items for maximum impact. For example, we added a label bearing a striking woven logo to the blankets for the Ivy Collection restaurants, emphasising the brand subtly and tastefully.

If your staff uniform has an own-brand garment tag, called a 'tax tab', you have the added advantage of being able to claim your VAT back because that is then considered as a business expense. No tax tab, no tax rebate: it's as simple as that.

Once you have your designs, get approval from a core focus group. Test your designs for fit, feel and style until you and your focus group are completely happy with them. When your designs are ready to be set up for production, you then need to make sure you have a sustainable supply source. Your supplier needs to be able to manage repeat deliveries consistently, and even store a stock of uniforms in all sizes for you so you can reorder without having to wait for new garments to be produced. I'm sure you don't want to go to all the effort of investing in creating your perfect design only to discover that it's no longer available to the same standards and at the same price when you come to reorder.

The whole supply chain needs to be robust, ethical, reliable, and tried and tested for quality. Look for suppliers who are recommended by people you know, like and trust, especially if they are in a similar industry to yours. A strong relationship with your designers and suppliers will mean you will get support when you need flexible options at short notice. If you represent loyalty and repeat business to them, they will likely find ways to save you both time and money, and there's a good chance they will place you high up on their priority list, not to mention the fact that they will have the knowledge and expertise on your exacting product and sourcing requirements embedded into their history, so you won't have to reinvent the wheel, but will be able to have your product, uniform or collection supply consistently enhanced because they have your back. It's all about trust and value.

Work with a designer who knows their supply chain well. This makes sure that any tweaks or updates of features, fibres or design can be done seamlessly. You also want to know that the supplier will deliver to your door with no hidden extra costs and that their prices aren't going to change each season. Have a deal with your chosen supplier for at least a minimum of two years. Customers who really value us see us as partners in building their brand and as a cornerstone of their brand supply chain, keeping their brand touch points strong. So look on your suppliers as your partners for the long term: that way everybody gets better value and gives more in return – and you get more in return. The more set in stone your deal is, the more time and money you will save. Having suppliers you can trust provides you with invaluable peace of mind, leaving you free to focus on doing what you do best, whether that's serving food, managing people, or launching a new product range.

INFLUENCE

Your uniform and signature products reinforce your brand values. A number of studies have shown the impact a uniform can have on a brand.

The Sawyer Business School, part of Suffolk University in Boston, carried out a study on whether uniforms are an effective marketing tool. When the study was carried out, it was already a recognised fact that uniforms are an important component of a hospitality establishment's brand identity, so the report dug deeper. It explained how a company can enhance its customers' knowledge about its brand through marketing initiatives. Gifts, stylish uniforms and branded products all create brand awareness among customers, resulting in their loyalty and a strong positive attitude towards the brand, naturally increasing their purchase activity.

When your brand is supported by assets (style, ethos, environment, culture, image, materials, value-added products and people, gifts and services) that resonate with your typical customer, it impacts everything and everyone. Internally, your staff feel more connected. There is less of a barrier between customer, employee and employer, the result being that everyone feels more relaxed. This naturally elevates service and up-selling, creating a tribe of loyal followers. Profits rise with regular repeat business and increased spend per customer. Staff stay loyal to your business and brand which saves a fortune in the financial and resource cost of staff turnover, re-training and time wasting. Retaining key talent is a perennial problem in the hospitality industry, and building a brand that staff can connect with is vital.

'Once someone has been with you for a few seasons and has experienced several cycles, that knowledge becomes valuable. They are able to use what worked and didn't work to inform decisions for the future planning, sales and service to great effect. That can't be bought, so the longer teams are happy and thriving, the better for the business. With women particularly, they need to be made to feel safe and secure in their roles to really thrive.'

Jackie Hay
Former Vice-President of Retail for Michael Kors

Research conducted by the Sawyer Business School shows how important it is to get your uniforms in place as a priority: over three quarters of respondents said that uniforms were more important than billboard advertising, and over half saw them as more effective than internet advertising.[†]

So, uniforms can carry more weight as a branding tool than many traditional forms of advertising, and when they're designed beautifully, they can elevate your brand's perceived quality, too.

IDENTITY AND IMPRESSION

Uniforms and unique textile touches help you stand out. Have you ever been to a shop or a restaurant and not been able to identify who works there? Who to speak with when you need help? I've even heard of someone, dressed in their smart clothes for a night out with friends, being mistaken for a member of the restaurant staff by a group of diners because the real staff were so difficult to identify. In short, it's frustrating.

You only have seven seconds to make a first impression, so make it count. A good first impression can be the difference between becoming a brand that is instantly recognised and losing a sale, and it is easy to create if your people and places shine.

† https://www.unifirst.com/pdf/uniforms-as-advertising.pdf

Look at how successful private members' clubs such as Soho House are, exporting their brand of coolness across the globe. These brands create a home from home, and once they get theirs members' loyalty, they generally keep it for life. Loyalty pays – by subscription, in the case of members' clubs. I would never question stopping my club membership to the Hospital Club. I love being part of a creative and quirky tribe who are also very open and welcoming.

A study entitled 'The Effect of Employee Uniforms on Employee Satisfaction', by Kathy Nelson and John Bowen, stated that uniforms clarify service. Apparently, staff who wear uniforms are more conscious of their actions. They are also much keener to set a good example for others. Interesting, hey?

According to marketing professor Victoria Seitz from California State University, San Bernardino, beautiful clothes can result in employees becoming aligned with their company. This ultimately leads to them becoming great assets for the company and increasing employee loyalty. The Hospital Club, for example, has a dress code for its reception staff which is quirky, stylish and cool. Rob Seals, the operations director, says the tone has been set by one particular member of the reception staff, Paul, who totally encompasses the Hospital Club's brand style.

'If you can't think how our dress code actually looks,' Rob adds, 'just look at Paul, who has it mastered.'

Sometimes, though, a brand can't just give its employees a uniform or a dress code; it has to follow this up with style dos and don'ts, tips on correct posture, and how to make eye contact with customers so employees can communicate their credibility.

VALUE

Making sure your staff look and feel valued is important. An attractive uniform or dress code and surroundings that display your brand identity can enhance your staff's self-esteem, which in turn improves staff morale. When they feel more valued, staff stay longer, and happy, settled staff encourage customers to return again and again. Conversely, an ill-fitting, ugly uniform will certainly not evoke confidence in your staff.

I was talking to a great leader from the Institute of Hospitality, Sarah Peters, whose early years in hospitality were in a family-run hotel business. The family decided to add a personal touch to the aprons, and Sarah hand embroidered each one with the initials of the hotel. To her surprise, the staff loved this unique textile touch so much that they made an effort to iron their aprons more beautifully than the owners had seen before. When people take ownership of their appearance, they care for their garments better.

It's important to have a 'unique to you' uniform that expresses your brand perfectly. If your uniform stands out in a stylish and timeless way, you will not need to redesign it for many years – unless, of course, you want to – and it will continue to look great. It also has to have the perfect fit for every individual, be practical and easy to care for, requiring little maintenance, and make your staff feel and look good wearing it for up to twelve hours. If you add to this good suppliers who can provide you with a sustainable resupply at the press of a button whenever you want the same uniform again, you are on to a winner.

I recently went to the Chelsea branch of a new and growing group of seriously high-end restaurants. The bar was just starting up as it was mid-morning. As I waited for my coffee, I had a good look around as I am a people watcher and style policer. Unfortunately, it's impossible for me to un-see the things I notice, and on this particular morning, I was shocked to see several of the bar staff were in oversized waistcoats. Many of the waistcoats already looked grubby even though the staff had only just started their shifts. It made me feel sad to think of all the lovely front-of-house girls in their stylish dresses, while the floor and bar staff were in cheap-looking and uncared-for attire. I've no doubt the people responsible for buying and supplying the uniforms never had to wear them, and the poor staff engagement and high staff turnover that probably resulted from this lack of appreciation meant that exquisite uniforms would not be seen as important.

2.1 – An employee selling premium wine in a poor uniform.

If your staff are embarrassed to be seen in their uniforms, the chances are that they will not make an effort, either in their work or in their appearance. They will likely want to hide, or even worse, leave the business and go to work for someone who cares about keeping staff supported, stylish, fit for purpose and happy. It's a very subtle thing but it made me notice and if I did, I'm sure many others would too. It prompts the subconscious question, 'Do they really care here?'

FOCUS GROUPS

If your staff are involved in choosing the uniform they will wear, you will end up with a positive, well-considered design that reflects your team culture. By including your staff in the decision-making process, you do two things: you let the staff know they are important and that their opinions matter, which does wonders for staff morale and self-esteem, and you create a build-up of excitement. Staff will look forward to being a part of each stage of their uniforms' design and production process, and who doesn't love being in on a secret?

Make sure you trial the fit and feel of the garment across a diverse group of staff, as everyone's body is different. You may think this is obvious, but so many directors or managers have left this role to the marketing/HR department. These departments in turn have ordered the entire production run from a catalogue or flat drawings without ever seeing a single sample or fabric swatch, let alone trying the uniforms on real people.

Some questions to ask of your focus group are:

- Is the fabric a good weight?
- Does it move in the right places?
- Is it comfortable?
- How does the style look on large women/men and those who are pencil thin or very short?
- Do the men's uniform and women's uniforms go together even though they are slightly different?
- What are your first impressions? Do you love it? Like it? Instincts really count.
- Is it fit for purpose?
- Would you want to wear it outside work? This is an important litmus test – you want your staff to love wearing their uniform and feel proud of it so they own their style.
- Is it on brand?
- Does it set the right tone?
- Are you proud of/confident in the uniform?
- Is there anything that could be improved/changed?
- Does the fit and style suit men's bodies?
- Does the fit and style suit women's bodies?
- Are there the right amount of size options?
- How could the design be scaled to accommodate unique body shapes while keeping its core style?

The ultimate result that you want is for staff to feel proud of their uniform and really love it. If they feel like they fit in with their work environment and feel in command when they're serving customers or speaking to important people, you have got it right.

MAKE YOUR BRAND SOUGHT AFTER

The Victoria and Albert Museum (V&A) in London has a design-led gift shop, and the gifts are great. I love buying unique designs that are special, beautiful and useful for people, and I'm also a sucker for quality memorabilia.

More and more companies with strong brands have seen the value of add-on sales merchandise, perhaps a business gift or an inexpensive purchase item from the capsule range that flies the flag of the brand. Most of these, interestingly, are textile-related items: a bag, a scarf, a tie, a keyring, cufflinks, or even a teddy with the branding on it.

I recently did some work for a not-for-profit association with a database of 10,000+ members, which is growing all the time. The association has hundreds of visitors every day, and they all tend to want something unique that they can take away to remember their experience by. We had to consider all the demographics of the members, guests and visitors. They are both male and female, young and old, very traditional and are family members of young barristers being called to the bar. Also a huge amount of tourists who want to see the history of this ancient place from the 16th century. It is a big deal to these guests to be connected to the association via a son or daughter, for example. So at the members' request, the association needed a merchandise range of distinction and diversity.

We started by designing a barrister's outfit for a teddy bear – adorned with the association's branding, of course. We also put together a tie range for male Alumni members and a pashmina range for the females. We then produced key rings, tie pins and cuff links, all carefully designed to be commercial, the highest quality and on brand.

British brands have so much that is worth accentuating, so it's important to do your brand justice. However, often businesses are too busy to appoint a specific person to do this. Branded items that remind people of their experience with the company are seen as add-ons rather than essential and core to the success of the business. These items are powerful touchpoints that ripple both internally and externally, so by offering a range of unique bespoke items, all carrying your branding clearly and stylishly, you can make your business, brand or association stand out.

It is wise to engage a design and product expert to work with you and report to you. Get them to do the legwork of designing, sourcing, costing and eliminating, according to your product list, selling price points and ethics, at the development stage. This will speed up the process by years and help you avoid expensive mistakes and brand damage. You don't want to get the quality and supply chain wrong through lack of expertise in this area. Once you are on a role with your brand extension, you can expand your creative vision and profits by co-creating with your chosen sourcing and design partner.

SUMMARY

We have covered a great deal in this chapter, so before we move on to the next stage of my personal journey through the wonderful world of style, let's have a quick recap.

If you have engaged staff, you will have happy customers. Happy customers remain loyal, which naturally increases profits. One of the best ways to engage your staff is to involve them in the design of their uniforms. If the uniform fits well, looks good and represents the values your brand stands for, your staff are likely to feel proud to wear it and far more confident in their work. Best of all, they will take ownership of their appearance. It is a proven fact that staff who like their uniforms take care of those uniforms – and what better way to make sure they like their uniforms than to involve them in the design stages?

Once you have your unique brand style, make sure it runs through everything associated with your brand, from the environment to the merchandise. A bespoke gift is a lovely way of giving your customers a memento of their time with you.

When designing and producing your brand's style, you need to make sure you work with experts. Ask people you trust and find out which designers and suppliers they would recommend. Consult an expert designer or consultant and engage them to take the stress out of creating your branded products. A little investment of time and money at the beginning of any project can save you a huge amount further down the line, so always take the time to source the best you can find. And most importantly, make sure everything is on brand: review the brand products and merchandise collections to see how they can be re-tweaked. It can be helpful to engage a brand consultant at this stage to oversee improvements to your brand quality and feel, and to keep enhancing your brand offering.

CHAPTER THREE

Embarking On A Designer's Life

After I'd spent five fantastic years with English Eccentrics, my boyfriend at the time got a job in Hong Kong. It was his first serious job as he had been struggling to get work as an architect in London, and I jumped at the opportunity to go with him on an adventure in Hong Kong, too. My dream by then was to work with Vivienne Westwood, but I had been putting this on hold as I was having such a lovely time with English Eccentrics, stretching and challenging myself in my quest to become a designer not just a product developer and production person, I wanted to be the full package!

My boyfriend and I left the UK for Hong Kong at the end of 1997, just after the transfer of sovereignty from Britain to China. While wanting to experience the same feeling of quality and community that I'd enjoyed with

English Eccentrics, I had my heart set on working for Shanghai Tang, a company with a unique style combining traditional Chinese clothing with a simple bold twist. Shanghai Tang knew who its target market was – the expat and designer market.

In January, shortly after I had arrived, it was Hong Kong fashion week. With no job, but a bag full of confidence and ambition and a thirst for adventure, I went to the Hong Kong Convention Centre and I registered myself as a free-lance designer, commissioned to source on behalf of English Eccentrics. *Well, I'll get to know some people here,* I thought. I remember being blown away by how entrepreneurial the new world of Hong Kong was. Some of the manufacturing companies seemed excited that I was a British designer; they said they were interested in having more British designers to present in their showrooms. I suddenly saw opportunities all around me to swing both ways – remain loyal to my British values while building connections overseas. It was an epiphany moment for me.

IMPORTING AND EXPORTING

At that time, I had just bought a book about how to be an exporter and importer of textiles in Hong Kong. David Birnbaum's *Importing Garments through Hong Kong: A Guide for the Perplexed* is the most inspiring and challenging book I've ever read about the business, and I keep it in my studio to this day. It taught me all about import VAT, duty, quota and shipping costs, and made me realise there is a bigger game to experience in global fashion, design, sourcing and manufacturing.

It was the steepest learning curve I have ever been through. I had to relearn how manufacturing was done, as in Hong Kong it has a completely different scale, quality and process to manufacturing in the UK. I discovered how to be more of an importer with a one-stop shop inside a factory. I just needed to give my partners within the factory the inspiration, design and measurements I wanted, and they would find where to source everything I required, from haberdashery detail and embellishment to embroidery, knitting, printing, weaving, sourcing ready-made fabric and dying. I loved the freedom and the limitless design techniques and manufacturing possibilities that this provided.

It appeared limitless, things I had found in charity shops all those years ago that were made beautifully, double knit reversible cardigans to incredible jacquard fabrics that I have never quite been able to find again were all available in this gigantic new shop window called Hong Kong and the gateway to Asia sourcing. There was real skill and expertise and artisans craft going on in all these different regions and you just had to suggest what you were looking for and these incredibly resourceful people in Hong Kong would find it.

Before long, I realised I was at a crossroads in my career. Not wanting to turn my back on British manufacturing and fashion, I also wanted to keep this incredible new world I had just discovered in my life so that I would have the freedom to have resources that I could use to make anything from a beautiful brooch to a jumper available at my fingertips through my Hong Kong agent or my factory partners. Where I could I made in England but there were just new things like crochet or beading from India that were much better to source where the detailed work was a speciality.

My first full-time job in Hong Kong was as head of ladies' wear for a sourcing office that supplied Jaeger, Monsoon and many other UK high-street brands. At that time, Hong Kong suppliers did all the 'middle-man' heavy lifting, merchandising and supplying for the industry. They were able to buy in finished items as completed units instead of using the cut, make and trim (CMT) model that the UK used, and the quality was excellent. However, I discovered I didn't much like supplying the high-street retailer because the fabrics were less luxurious. We had to choose polyesters (when polyester was not so beautiful or clever) and less quality materials and quite generic textile designs that were not designer quality, and we had to push hard for the best possible prices. I had been used to silks, devoré velvet and artisans' embroideries hand-crafted in India, and other beautiful fabrics which were unique and of timeless high quality.

THE LONDON CONSULTANCY

While I was in Hong Kong, I had been planning to build my own brand, manufacturing directly with factories based there and selling to the UK market that I knew so well. I went to work for a couple of manufacturing and sourcing houses as a part-time designer, using the rest of the time to work on my own brand and developments from their offices. I was very excited by the opportunity, but unfortunately I was soon to discover that I had endometriosis and needed to have surgery in the UK. My relationship ended around that time, too, so I never went back to live in Hong Kong, and it wasn't until 2003 that I would finally build my own luxury ladies' wear label. Back in the late nineties, though, my focus was all on my new plan – a London-based consultancy.

Having returned to the UK from Hong Kong after two years away and recovered from my surgery, I immediately saw a niche in the UK market. There was an opportunity to supply luxury level brands with tailored products using a pool of factories whose work was tried and tested, and with whom I'd built strong relationships. These factories were prepared to produce small quantities – fifty pieces or fewer per style.

With my designer's eye looking out for techniques, trims and materials that matched my clients' brand styles, the service could include rich and varied sourcing which would take their resources to a new level of choice. It was a very exciting and liberating time for everyone involved. My clients suddenly had the resources of global brand complexity and quality, and often it was the first time they'd had the opportunity to make something outside of the UK.

3.1 – My best selling 'Rose Dress' from my first collection of Forever Young.

While I was in Hong Kong, I gathered together a wealth of tried and tested contacts, resources and disciplines. To this day, I still work with many of my connections, along with the many more I have developed since. I treasure my business connections, and as a result, I have become an avid connector of people. Part of my passion and creativity stems from connecting people through fashion.

CONNECTING PEOPLE THROUGH FASHION IN THE UK

Once I was well again and settled back in UK, I launched my design and sourcing consultancy from London, working with luxury brands that exhibited at London Fashion Week. These brands included my old friends at English Eccentrics, along with La Petite Salope, Billy Bag, Goya, Britt Lintner, and Johnny Loves Rosie, to name but a few.

As I built up my work, I also took on private commissions for celebrity clients such as Toyah Wilcox, and for brides, grooms, bridesmaids, mothers of the bride, friends and CEOs, all wanting to have unique bespoke outfits created for them. I gathered together a handful of skilled tailors, machinists and pattern cutters on a freelance basis to fulfil my orders. The variety of clients and projects was wonderful – I loved it.

In addition, I consulted for brands as a sourcing agent, helping them find factories, fabrics and manufacturers as they scaled their businesses up. Many of these brands were working with individual outworkers dotted all over London or making orders themselves, all the while struggling to grow a designer fashion brand. Having a proper manufacturing system and technical specs in place helped these brands create more space and capacity, thrive, and focus on their amazing products and brands, rather than the back end, sample development and production.

During my career as a sourcing agent/consultant, I took many representatives of the brands I worked with on tours of Hong Kong, introducing them to my partners there to help them to develop their products. It worked really well for many years, and even though there were some steep learning curves along the way, these provided me with more and more valuable experience of importing and production – experience which I can rely on to this day in challenging situations. As I was the one who made sure everything got sorted, I had to build partnerships with people who could help problem solve.

SUMMARY

My time in Hong Kong taught me that there was a completely different manufacturing model outside the UK, with a far more joined-up approach. It also revealed to me that there was a role for me in consultancy, in making all the scattered outworkers producing their exquisite tailoring or accessories more accessible to brands already wholly occupied in developing their hallmark and their clientele.

The key to making this work was developing strong and productive partnerships – an approach that will take you a long way in any line of business.

Now let's get on to the practicalities of building your bespoke uniform, product ranges and signature style.

CHAPTER FOUR

Creating a
Signature Style

Most people cannot find what they really want in the shops, so put up with whatever is the best they can get for their budget. This can mean a lot of waste and over-consuming as they go on endless quests for something stylish and different. I experienced this frustration at an early age when I needed to buy outfits for both my mum's and my dad's weddings to their new partners. I struggled to find a style that suited the occasion and looked good on my body shape.

Fashion can actually lead people well away from what is best for them, leaving them dispirited and confused. The secret is to discover what suits you, and that starts with knowing your body shape.

PROPORTIONS

Everyone's body is different, so you need to know your body proportions to find a brand that fits you well. Once you know your ideal brands and styles that suit you best, you can then break the style rules to suit you.

Of course, where you shop personally to suit your body shape is not going to be perfect for everyone. To discover what will best accommodate your staff or customers, study the lines and the types of shapes that work best for your body shape, and take that as a standard. Then you need to look at how your staff's body shapes differ to the standard you have set to see where to use the BESPOKE™ principles (which we will cover in detail in Chapter 5) to adapt the standard to fit everyone.

Fit is critical to the uniform looking flattering on both you and your staff. Once you have a good cross section of the variations in body shape of your team, you can put a scaled ratio of size options together. For example, if you have a mixture of tall bodies, short bodies and average height bodies on your team, you could create three back length options in your desired styles.

Knowing how best to enhance your body shape means you need to recognise the parts that you like and those that you don't like, then find styles to enhance your favourable features. And the same goes for your staff. It's all about making you and your team look and feel good, and fit is a fundamental part, usually overlooked – but it can make the most significant difference if you have a designer in charge of overseeing how they fit on your staff's bodies.

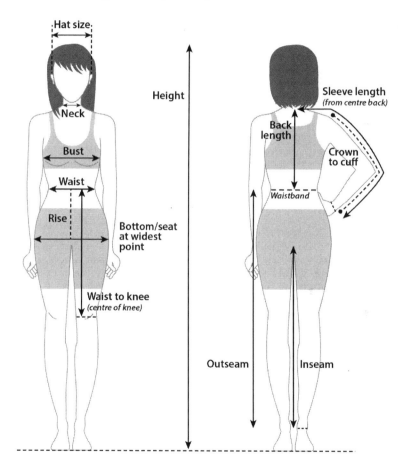

4.1 – Diagram of back length variations.

If you have a long back and short legs, go for longer proportions on the legs and waist or a high hip-length top. Make sure
the waist height of the top is not too short, or if it is, avoid it
being nipped in at the waist, otherwise it will look like it's too
high up on your body and the hips are not fitting correctly.

For a short back length and long legs, you need to have
short-waisted tops so they don't sit too low on the waist,
because then the likelihood is they won't fit properly on
women's hips, either. If your widest point is at the hips,
don't wear tops that finish on the hips, and wear the same
colour or tones if possible for a slimming effect.

If a woman's bust is large, I would suggest an open blouse
neckline, a V neck or a scoop neckline to draw the eye down.
Creating a V makes large-breasted women look less busty.
Drawing attention to the waist area with a seam or detail is
only flattering if the waist is small. If it's wide, go for vertical
lines to lengthen the proportion.

4.2 – The measuring points on a body.

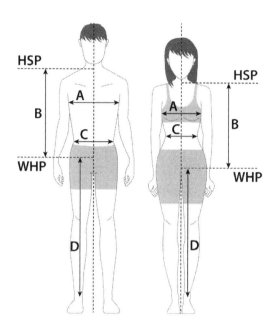

A	Chest Width
B	Body Length from HSP to WHP
C	Waist Width
D	Inside Leg Length
HSP	Highest Shoulder Point
WHP	Widest Hip Point

A. Measure the chest around the fullest part, place the measuring tape close up under the arms making sure the tape is well up at the back over the shoulder blades

B. Measure the body length from the HSP to the top of the hip, where the hem for a top will naturally sit. Make sure the back is straight

C. Measure the waist around the natural waistline; this will be close to the bellybutton. Put one finger between the tape and the body before taking the measurement

D. Measure the inside leg from the groin to the lower ankle

HOW TO DESIGN FOR MULTIPLE BODY SHAPES AND STYLES

Understanding the practical purpose of each item of clothing you and your staff will wear and the brand identity values it needs to reflect or embody is essential.

- What is the customer market level?
- Is the garment meant to last a long time?
- What does it have to fit in with?

You can use colour, shape and texture interwoven into the style features of a practical use item. For example, my team and I built up a signature offering of napkins for a high-end hospitality client. The napkins were designed using a key colour from the client's environment and interiors, and that colour was interwoven into check and jacquard patterns. This was so successful for their flagship restaurants that they then duplicated it as a textile touch point for all the future restaurants that they opened. While always keeping ivory on napkins and grey on the aprons as the base colour, they would change one or two of the contrast colours. For example, they complemented the grey with a green on the reverse of the aprons, or used grey and petrol blue, or grey and burnt orange, on their other sites. These colour schemes used with the same consistent branding linked the new restaurants to their 'parent' sites, but textile colour twists gave each new site separate stand-out brand features, making it unique.

When you're accommodating the diverse needs of staff to find clothing that best suits all, the simplest way to do it is to take one gender at a time. Ask questions to dig deep, for example, 'How important a role is this uniform going to have?' Remember, you only have seven seconds to make a first impression, so you need to know what each member of staff is going to be unconsciously saying to your customers and prospects through their attire.

Women. What does the clothing brief need to deliver? Is it to be feminine, modern, minimalistic, classic, or retro in style? What are the influences in the brand that need to be highlighted in the uniform? What are all the practical needs of that uniform to perform at its best and still look great?

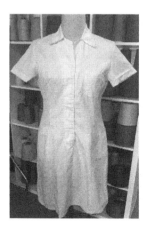

4.3 – Previous not fit for purpose uniform we were briefed to redesign and improve.

4.4 – Working toile of the re-designed uniform solution that is more stylish and timeless.

Is it two pieces or a dress? Does it need a cardigan or jacket, tabard, or apron?

Look at practicality, diversity, comfort, whether the uniform is for front or back of house (or both), performance, and type of style. You are looking to create a uniform for optimum flattery which needs to be multipurpose in most cases and a universal style. The universal style means you can bring your collection or uniform to the masses.

Men. There are similar questions to ask when you are designing a uniform for men:

- Is it to be smart or casual?
- What is it to fit with?
- What is its role?
- Are you focusing on tops or shirts or is there a jacket required, too?
- Are trousers being provided? Many uniforms these days actually include informal trousers being worn and supplied by the employee. Providing the jacket and the top or the shirt and sometimes the shoes can add distinctive style features.
- What are the care, quality, brand and ethics requirements?
- Who is going to be cleaning it, the staff member or the company? It's very important it can be easily taken care of to look at its best when somebody not particularly experienced at looking after clothes or textiles has to clean it.

Generic clothing. For an apron, I always advise going for knee length or shorter so you have minimum proportion and practicality issues. This length suits most people, whether they are tall or short, slim or wide. Adding an adjustable strap around the neck helps to accommodate people of all sizes.

Half aprons tied at the waist are popular. Adding a detail of bespoke embroidery will make it instantly recognisable as a part of your brand, and will be tax deductible – a win-win. Many of my clients opt for grey or navy as they both suit all skin types, it's always fashionable, and blends well if you make interior or brand changes.

4.5 – Dirty Burger aprons, a Soho House restaurant brand.

Tops. T-shirts and shirts are best if you get them semi-fitted. My recommendation is to go for Lycra blended material to give it the flexibility to stretch.

A common mistake with tops is to go for a large T-shape or an oversized shirt or item that drowns small staff and makes them feel inadequate, and doesn't flatter large people, either. There is nothing worse than seeing somebody in an oversized top, it looks like they haven't been able to find something or are hiding something and both provoke strange questions in your subconscious mind, so don't do it to your staff. In today's style-conscious world, tailored clothing shows you've thought about fitting and flattering staff of all sizes and ages. Again, you then add bespoke branding, choosing colours wisely.

For both men and women, accommodating for petite, regular, and long bodies can be challenging, so semi-fitted can help with that, too. I encourage a curved hem as it can be tucked in or out at the mid to low hip and still flatter almost every body shape. I also recommend a minimum of five standard tops sizes.

TAILORING

My lovely stylist Kaye told me that oversized clothing with long sleeves that go over the knuckle make people look and feel inferior. For that reason, I tend to steer clients towards petite jackets. I would always say that if somebody's sleeve length is too long get it altered at your local dry cleaners. Any company can do that if your uniform supplier can't bespoke those items for you. For women, go for a three-quarter-length sleeve, which is flattering and practical. Jackets add authority and rank, and can elevate staff's behaviour, so when they're well made and styled, they enhance performance and provide professionalism. I always wear a jacket for important meetings, and sometimes even in my studio when I'm making calls or doing admin work. It makes me feel clearer and more focused.

There are many more design features available that I will cover later in the book. For now, simply realise that the more you can make each staff member feel unique even though you are giving them a uniform, it shows you have thought about each individual with the fit and provided a practical, purposeful style that will also have longevity for the wearer and the brand. This ultimately sustains your identity and helps to keep your people with you for the long term.

FABRICS

Use fabrics that are fit for purpose, durable and are as sustainable as possible. If we're talking about napkins, use a mix of linen, ramie and cotton, or pure cotton. These fabrics are robust and stand up well to continuous washing.

Bamboo is a good option, too: the quality feels nice and natural to the customer. Bamboo is also antibacterial so it self-cleans, which is a win twice over for the environment, as it is also an unbelievably sustainable plant that grows quicker than we can actually consume it. The higher the thread count, the more refined and long lasting, but also the more expensive the fabric will be.

With clothing, my approach would be a blended one. You want a fabric to perform, hold its colour, give comfort, and be breathable. It's a balancing act between blends of fibre and construction that fit your requirements as well as being stylish and interesting. If you're a novice, I would advise you to look at content labels inside clothing or on products that you like for ideas on what you want to be similar to. This can sometimes give you an indication as to where to source the material and/or product and where it can be made easily, too.

For example, notice if the cotton used in the material is grown in Turkey, Pakistan or India. It may well be that it can be woven into fabric close to its place of origin. I like to work with the artisans and manufacturers that are most familiar with working on that material, like cotton. Also, I tend to look for manufacturing which is also close to where the factory is as a way of cutting down logistics. it saves costs, saves time and saves on lack of experienced handlers. Silk is made from silkworm cocoons and is tradi-tionally and easily sourced in China, Thailand and Vietnam where this material has been made and traded from for thousands of years since before the silk route was discovered. Working with silk is an ancient craft of these countries; in each region you are likely to find speciality silks and artisans, as well as commercial and sustainable enterprises for larger orders.

BLENDING AND SUSTAINABILITY

When I'm talking to my clients about uniform or textile durability, I tend to recommend a sustainable natural fibre like cotton or bamboo as a base. I then recommend blending this with polyester (recycled polyester if you can get it) for three reasons:

- It helps the fabric to hold its colour
- It makes the fabric more durable
- It makes the fabric easier to care for

If your staff have a tendency not to iron their uniforms, the addition of polyester will noticeably lessen the creases.

You could also consider adding some stretch to your fabric using a fibre called spandex, which is more commonly known as Lycra. Lycra can be blended with most natural and man-made fibres, so I like to use it with silk and polyester where required. It's both practical and forgiving, and I'm

sure your staff will appreciate a bit of stretch in their clothing, especially if they have to sit down or bend over a lot.

If you don't require a vast number of garments, it doesn't
make sense to create your own bespoke fabric blend
and pattern. Instead, it is perfectly acceptable for you to
choose an off-the-shelf option. This option means your
order will be completed faster. In the short term or for
short-run orders, there is a huge variety of fabric suppliers for you to choose from, but this kind of deal may not
be sustainable because the same fabric may no longer be
available in the future.

Have a search on Google. Depending on your price point,
pretty much anything is available. The Offset Warehouse
is a fantastic resource to build a brand using end-of-
line designer fabrics, and plenty of similar mills exist,
too. Make sure the wholesalers and mills match your
couture, and are preferably located in the same country as
your factory.

Ask around at your factory to find out if people in the know
can recommend or source fabrics on your behalf. This will
make the whole process of finding your fabric much easier,
especially if you are not sure what you need. Alternatively,
send your factory a swatch of something you like, which
any good fabric retailer will supply. Most towns have fabric
shops, and if you're London based, you have a wealth of

choice. Berwick Street, Poland Street and Shepherd's Bush Market are excellent places to visit.

4.6 – Bill's reverse stripe half aprons.

4.7 – Use the Zappar app to scan the code and watch the video showing how our hospitality journey began.
https://www.youtube.com/watch?v=XgltiUHa_Fc

COLOURS

The most common colours in uniform design, and the ones that I believe work best, are navy and charcoal. They flatter all skin tones and don't tend to go out of fashion. Red is another colour which will work on many people, but I tend to use red for just one garment.

The colour you choose depends on your brand identity and ethos, the image you want to purvey, the impact and impression you are striving for, and how long you need the item to look great for. I love colour, and where possible I use highlights which complement an item of clothing. Blending a signature colour from your decor into your clothing or products works well to bring a brand together. This colour could be used for embroidery on table napkins or as a contrast colour on the reverse side of an apron.

BRINGING IT ALL TOGETHER

Let me illustrate how to bring together everything we've discussed in this chapter with an example. My client in this case was a hugely creative, inspiring restaurant group for middle-market young and family demographics. This group started with one site, but soon grew very quickly indeed.

The group decided it had had enough of its dreary, ill-fitting and completely inadequate off-the-shelf uniforms. The clothing didn't express its brand look, feel or ethos.

It's quite common in service industries generally not to have a nominated member of staff who knows how to source decent uniforms. The task usually gets foisted on to a project manager or procurement director, when really what the business needs is the support of an independent expert. It's unlikely that a project manager is going to know how to find designers who understand the business's brand, or supply chain solutions that meet the brand's ethics, budget and product/service requirements. These two components may not come from the same company, so collaboration with an expert is a good idea for most businesses.

On my initial visit to the restaurant group's head office, I met with the head of training, who had been tasked with the job of engaging a designer and supply solution for the new uniforms. From day one, I got the sense that he really understood what the staff needed in terms of comfort and had good ideas on the potential style for the brand, as he was deeply engaged with its heritage. It's unusual for someone to know exactly what staff are going to need and want to wear – right through to actually knowing how they want to be styled – because they've experienced being on the floor themselves. So it was great to work with this guy in this way, to marry up the needs and the design. To begin with, he definitely knew what the staff didn't like and what wouldn't work, and that was the perfect way to cut directly to looking at what would enthuse the staff.

The complaints that the staff had were as follows:

Shirts
- The cotton fabric was too heavy, so the staff were too hot most of the time
- The shirts were hard to iron, so the staff had to spend a lot of time ironing to get them to look half decent
- The women's shirts didn't fit well, resulting in the managers having to collate up the female staff in some of the sites to take the men's shirts to the tailor down the road. This added unnecessary hassle and expense to their managers' workload and head office budget
- The fabric had no give or stretch and would often start to look bulky over the course of a shift. It also tended to untuck at the waist when staff had been reaching over tables a lot
- The staff couldn't wait to get out of the shirts at the end of the shift as they were so uncomfortable and not something you wanted to be seen meeting your mates in
- The style was totally unsuitable for the group's demographic of staff, who were mainly young staff members who were either starting out their career or doing waitressing as a supplement to whatever else they were doing – like being an actor or studying – so something older, heavier and dated was not particularly great for their style moral

- They had no tax tab so were not legally a tax-deductible expense they could claim VAT back on

> Tip: Discover what your staff feel about their uniforms. What works and doesn't work for them? This is the most important first step when you're designing a new uniform. It gives you all the clues.

At the time, this client had twenty-five restaurants in total, each having on average twenty-five staff, and the group supplied three shirts per waiter. This made a total of 1,875 shirts (that's without the 30% surplus stock of various sizes for the natural staff turnover that happens in every hospitality business). The stock cost was huge, and the group had a growth plan to expand to twenty-five new sites that year, so it wanted to make sure the new uniforms would be a good investment that would last them both in terms of style and practicality for a long time. To invest heavily in the redesign and the resupply was going to be a tiny bit more expensive than buying off-the-shelf versions that didn't work and that were also wasting money – currently they were spending on a product that they were just going to have to dump or recycle.

Aprons
- They were too long and restrictive. More than half the staff were having to roll them up around the waist so as not to trip over them, making them look bulky
- They didn't have the company branding or a little tax tab anywhere as they were sourced from a standard off-the-shelf uniform brand
- The colour was not a bespoke colour matching their brand
- Most importantly of all, the staff didn't like them
- They had the brand of the uniform supplier displayed, which is possibly not what you really want to promote, especially if it's a low-end work wear brand

Once we had got the essential uniform briefing requirements of comfort, practicality and budget out of the way, we talked about style. We went back to my studio to pull together some story boards with style ideas, sketches, fabrics and detailing. The group was passionate about sharing the history of the brand and its founder. It had all started from a family greengrocer's shop, so the head of training told me he wanted to draw inspiration from the group's roots and add a contemporary look and feel with quirky retro touches to complement the brand's casual dining style.

Armed with this knowledge, I dug deeper during the design research process. I asked questions like:

- Do you want the men and women to look exactly the same or are you ok with them looking a little bit distinctive and different?
- What is your colour palette? What colour would you love?
- Can you sum up your core style/brand in three words?
- Do you have any examples or inspiration you'd like to share with me?
- Would you like a pattern, print or weave feature on the fabric?
- Do you have brand guidelines?
- What would your staff like/dislike?

Tip: If you have an idea of what you want but don't know how to get it, ask questions to clarify your thoughts and narrow down the way to go forward. I would advise creating a mood board to present the initial ideas of the design's look and feel, and act as a starting point when you're choosing fabric, print and shape. It's good to take inspiration from what's available, whether you're going for modern or retro.

We began to create a design for what they really wanted on a blank canvas, inspired by the answers to these questions. This gave us a chance to pull lots of research together to show how we could respond creatively through different features, but without committing at this stage to a completely finalised solution. This was just a starting point, to give them a design direction that we could really get some clear reactions to, enabling us to go on to the next stage.

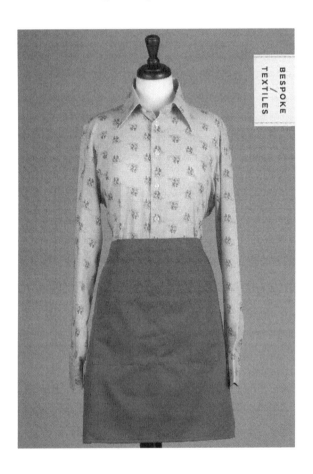

4.8 – Vintage shirt inspiration, styled with a modern half apron.

The head of training, the managers and some of the staff from head office and some of their restaurant sites were gathered together to look at the ideas. They loved it, they felt excited. They felt I had really captured the brand feel and the demographic that they served and that their employees were based on, which is a really important mirror that you need to get right for your brand. Rather than approaching the task as just designing a uniform, I had set about designing clothes people would love to wear.

> Tip: Engage a designer who understands people, fit and textiles well, and this understanding will translate into your brand.

Once I had come up with ideas and solutions to suit the people who were going to wear the uniforms, I briefed the fabric mill to come up with fabric blends and a design weave with the restaurant group's price point in mind. I then got the archive swatches out and went back to the client with a selection of fabrics to inspire them. We settled on a micro check which I wove up in a few colour combos, eventually narrowing the colour down to a charcoal and ivory print. This was practical as it wouldn't show sweat marks and gave the retro feel that the brand was looking for.

The next stages were to design sketches, select the ones the group liked, and then develop the shape. We made prototypes for both the men and the women.

The first prototypes were made with spandex woven into the fabric base for stretch. We then simply graded the sizes from small to medium and large for a trial focus group of twenty or so staff.

4.9 – Illustration of new uniform proposal.

By trialling the prototypes on a focus group, we were able to find out what the staff thought, looking for common themes and any unusual shapes we would need to accommodate. I got to speak to the end users of each uniform directly and hear what they thought about the fit, fabric and design, and how they would feel doing a twelve-hour shift in it. I requested that they tested all the typical movements they would need to make during their shift and asked questions like:

- Does the uniform feel comfortable?
- Can you move well in it?
- How does the fabric feel?
- Do you like it?
- How do you wear your sleeves, rolled up or down?
- Is there anything you would recommend changing? What could improve if we changed it?

This restaurant group encouraged its staff to be individuals. They had the freedom to wear their uniforms according to their own style, comfort and personality. Some rolled their sleeves up, others wore them down. Some buttoned their shirts at the neck, others wore them open necked. This sort of flexibility works well in casual dining, and in the case of the restaurant group, it really helped me design features around how the majority of staff would prefer to wear the uniform.

> Tip: Listening to the staff's needs and allowing them to bring individuality into the process pays dividends.

Outcome

- The uniform fabric was lightweight, breathable and comfortable, with stretch
- The staff really liked the check print and said that it was something they'd feel comfortable wearing outside work
- We decided on three-quarter-length sleeves for the ladies (who had always rolled their sleeves up on the old uniform) and full-length sleeves for the men
- The ladies had more bust shaping and darting as well as long body darts for an optimal flattering fit
- The men had a modest collar that looked great done up or undone, and gave a preppy look
- The men also had slight shaping at the sides and long body darts at the back to create slim-fitting shirts

> Tip: When you bring your staff together, you find they have all the answers. Pulling together the core people of a business and all of the design elements and information, you will achieve powerful decisions concerning the design process, and staff unity will increase as you will have removed any hierarchy issues.

THE PERILS OF AN IMPRACTICAL UNIFORM

I worked as a waitress from the age of thirteen in the local tourist leisure centre, and I continued to waitress for a bit of extra money throughout my years as a student. Even after I had moved to London and started working for English Eccentrics fashion house, I still worked a few evenings for an agency that booked me as a waitress for events.

The agency did not provide its waitresses with uniforms, just a dress code: we had to wear a black skirt, black tights, black shoes, and the agency supplied white shirts and dickie bow ties. I wore a heavy jersey tube-knit skirt I had made for waitressing as it was plain, comfortable, and in a classic pencil style, finishing just above the knee.

While waitressing, we had to have silver fork and spoon servers with us at all times. Most of the time, we would tuck them into our waistbands because that was the only practical place to keep them – we had no aprons issued to us.

On one particular night, the tables were set out across a football pitch-sized room. Once everyone was seated and the starters had been cleared, we were given a huge platter of potatoes to rest on one arm and a stack of ten oval plates to carry on the other. When everyone had these in hand, we all set off at once on the long walk from the kitchens and across the dining room.

As I got half way across the hall, I felt my silver serving fork and spoon starting to slip down from my waist. Oh dear!

But worse was to come. The white shirts the agency supplied were oversized to accommodate any man or woman. My shirt was far too big for me and had a 16-inch collar, but I'd simply been told to tuck it in and tighten the dickie bow tie around the neck if it annoyed me. I had tucked the vast amount of surplus material into my tights in an endeavour to flatten it, and naturally, my fork and spoon decided to slip into the inside of my tights, too. By the time I got to the table, I had a silver fork and spoon at my knee, nestling inside my tights for all to see.

I honestly thought I was about to drop everything. The entire table watched as one man reached out for the pota-toes and left me free to balance the plates on the table. As I was so far from the kitchen, there was no turning back. All I could do was reach down into my skirt, down into my tights, while still standing at the table, and pull the cutlery out. The guests then all watched in horrified fascination as I proceeded to serve the potatoes with the badly behaved fork and spoon. There was no other option – we had strict instructions to make sure we all served our allocated guests at the same time.

I stuck with my fashion alterations and commissions for extra money after that.

If you don't care for your staff's basic clothing needs to do their job, it can have disastrous results and really look bad on you too. All it takes is a little bit of planning and care. Imagine how you would feel if you had to go and perform in a professional environment, highly visible to VIPs and clients, and were told to wear something you felt uncomfortable, ugly and inferior in?

Make sure you are setting your staff up to win.

INVISIBLE INFLUENCES

Have you ever felt odd with certain people or in certain environments, but not known exactly why? Equally, has the reverse happened where you've felt drawn to certain people or environments, either online or physically?

When values and influences align, something magical happens. Being aligned applies to style, business, brands and individuals, and there are many unseen influences at work.

Many years ago, I had my distinctive style identified and developed by the fabulous stylist, Kaye. Kaye matches individuals to their style, and it was fascinating to me to see how layers of garments combine with colour tones, jewellery, makeup, and hairstyles to help people express themselves and empower their presence to the maximum. Kaye demonstrated this in reverse by taking each layer of her own style away one by one.

She removed her jacket, and in doing so removed the persona of authority and credibility it had created. She then ruffled and rolled up the sleeves of her shirt. She unbuttoned her shirt at the front, exposing more flesh at the neck. With these gestures, she no longer had the same formality, and her energy changed.

Taking off her earrings was like removing a medal of honour. Earrings are a subtle but powerful finisher. Her necklace had represented worth, polishing the outfit and look, and the belt had provided structure. Lastly, she wiped off her lipstick, making what she said seem less important, and without her eye makeup, she didn't look as sparkly, energetic and elegant.

It was like a penny dropping. Suddenly, I no longer related to her in the same way. That final removal of her makeup totally weakened her communication. It was amazing to see how subtle changes can make such a difference to how we behave and interact with others.

Think about all the elements of what you want to communicate with what you're wearing, because clothing, accessories and makeup have a big impact. Put a little effort into how you can add more value and gravitas to your look while making sure it's congruent with what you say, believe, and want to portray. If cool is your thing, make sure your look is pure quality, and embrace brand pairing – finding other brands that match your style and values – with cool brand elements. And, of course, the people skills of you and you staff need to match your brand ethos.

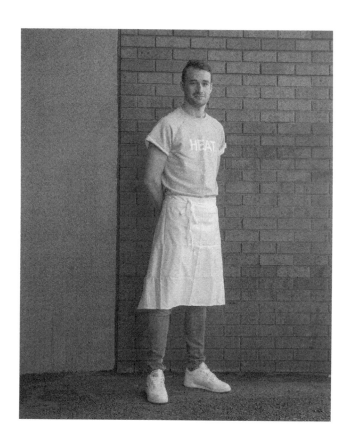

4.10 – Uniform styling for a London Hotel Restaurant.

In his book *The Invisible Influence*, Kevin Hogan writes about the 'Kim Kardashian effect'. This is one of the most fascinating invisible influences I have ever heard about.

Here's a little test. Think about your house name or number, street name, and company name. Do they contain similar letters or numbers? Do the letters or numbers sit closely together alphabetically or numerically? Are there repeated numbers, names or letters that come up in your life?

According to Kevin Hogan, the Kardashians built their brand using the power of the letter K as part of their tool kit. It's no surprise, then, that the family continued to attract other Ks, for example, when Kim Kardashian married Kanye West.

The Kardashian effect is a subtle thing, but once I started to notice it, I spotted it everywhere. So go with those magnetic nudges. There are many energetic forces at work, and they make the game of designing your brand merchandise and assets fun.

SUMMARY

In the next chapter, I am going to introduce you to BESPOKE™ Methodology, which encapsulates the principles I use when designing for myself or working with clients. Before we move on to that, though, let's have a quick recap of everything we've covered in this chapter.

When you're designing the perfect uniform to delight your staff and reflect your brand, it is important that you steer well clear of the dreaded one-size-fits-all approach. To my mind, that's a total misnomer – it should be one size fits *no one*. You need to take into account the different body shapes of your staff in the fit of your uniforms, and their different skin tones in the colour you choose. Also think about the practicality and sustainability of the fabric you use. What about pattern? What matches your brand values? Are you looking for modern or retro, casual or formal? What will make you staff proud to be seen in their uniforms?

A great idea is to get them involved. Ask them questions, and really listen to understand what they do and don't like. Look at their preferences – do they like to wear their sleeves rolled up or down? Their collars buttoned or open? Could accommodating their preferences match your brand values?

Think about the subtle touches. What accessories would help to emphasise your brand's message? Would jackets, ties or belts enhance your staff's impact? Would the power of a certain letter or number give consistency to your brand? Your staff's uniform is an essential part of your brand, but too many companies fail to treat its design with the importance it deserves. If you have no one in-house who can source the correct fabrics and designers, work with an expert to make sure you get it right and set your staff up to win.

Design clothes and products that people really want to wear or buy, that you would really love, as well as the demographic that you are serving. Don't default to thinking 'we just need to have a uniform' or 'we just need to have some cushions' or 'we just need to have a t-shirt with a logo'. Think more creatively than that – as if you were designing clothes to last a lifetime.

CHAPTER FIVE

The Bespoke
Principle

How can you achieve bespoke touches that mirror your brand values in your business? I follow the principles I have developed in my work, style, home, life and sourcing in the process of evolving a design or product. It's essential that the ethos and values of a brand are carried through from the initial concept to the fully tailored supply chain.

5.1 – Use the Zapper app to scan the code and watch the video of me talking about the top uniform problems and the BESPOKE™ Methodology.
https://www.youtube.com/watch?v=tnl5KR6RZcs

The BESPOKE™ principles are an invaluable resource to help you apply these touches to all your textile creations.

The BESPOKE™ acronym stands for:

- Beauty
- Ethics
- Style
- People
- Organisation
- Kindness and karma
- Endless sustainable supply

Let's have a look at each one in detail.

B: BEAUTY

To develop your first prototype, you could start by taking inspiration from your existing garments or items, or you could choose a garment or item that you want to replicate or that evolves, and use this as a starting point. Discover what you and your staff love and what you don't like so that you can drill down to what your new creation needs to incorporate. What essence, properties and practicalities do the items need to have? Gather the ideas together on a mood board using pictures, material swatches, photos and magazine references, then narrow everything down to create a story.

When your unique ideas reveal themselves, your bespoke beauty journey will have begun.

I love to take inspiration from vintage clothing because the cut and shape is usually so interesting. There is an abundance of underused ideas waiting to be evolved from the past. Mass manufacture only took off in the late 1950s/early 1960s, so there was no ready-to-wear clothing available prior to that time. Most people wore homemade, tailored or designer clothing. Garments were much more considered, unique to body shapes, and well made.

My inspiration and influences come mainly from the forties, fifties, sixties and seventies, and I have collected an archive of garments and materials from these eras in particular. My favourite piece is a vintage men's sample shirt which I have kept as a reference point for a good fit and the retro styling of fabric and prints. In fact, I used it as the inspiration for the men's shirt shape when I was working with the Bill's restaurant chain to redesign its uniforms.

It is my passion to collect unique items from travels and markets, and find interesting old designer labels. By sketching, collaging and putting things together, from napkin embroidery to a type of seaming, you too can build beautiful and timeless style ideas for yourself and/ or your brand.

E: ETHICS

When it comes to buying or making uniforms, clothes, or any textile item for that matter, do you consider where the clothing came from and how it was made? People are becoming increasingly fascinated with and educated on how and where the products they buy were produced. If it's a food product, is it organic? What's the product's journey? If your restaurant sources its food ethically, it makes sense to extend that approach to the rest of your business, including textiles. Customers like a holistic approach when it comes to the brands they use and will expect the brand's values and ethics to be reflected across all its components.

Know where, how and by whom your uniforms are made. Brands that care are perceived in a better light by consumers than those that don't, and if your uniforms are sourced ethically and made from sustainable materials, it can increase you customer approval. This is invaluable, as if they resonate with your brand, customers are more likely to spend money with you and become loyal. Decide on the right fit for your business, from the suppliers to the products to the service, and create a balance of values against financial gain.

In both the fast fashion and hospitality industries, there is huge pressure to make everything cost-effective, although the higher end brands of both these industries are investing more into sustainable values and standards. I usually find that I need to educate people in this area so that they know what customers truly want and how this will maintain the value of their brand, as well as the costings, without cutting corners. As a consumer, I would absolutely want to know whom I'm dealing with through the brands I use and what's important to them, no matter how big (or small) their teams are. Are we on the same page?

One of my clients was so dedicated to treating their customers and suppliers equally, with the same values and services, that they created a *Handbook of Ethics* for the staff. New recruits were given the handbook and immediately felt like they were joining a family, and I found that really inspiring.

However, sometimes executives in a company can forget the brand's values when number crunching issues come up.

Imagine the following scenario, for example. Your company has been working with an expert for five months, developing designs and prototypes, refining the designs, and working on multiple sampling stages. You have held a number of staff focus group fittings to create the perfect size templates. The fabric you've decided on is unique to your brand, created with three different fibres to suit your staff's practical needs.

The moment you are finally ready for bulk production, pending the directors' sign off on the order quantity, you have a holiday booked. While you are away, the managing director takes your samples and contacts an old supplier he worked with previously. By the time you return from your holiday, the managing director has decided the uniforms are going to be made by this other company, the reasons being that it is offering a slightly lower price point and longer credit terms. All your hard work developing a uniform that would perfectly demonstrate the brand's values and ethics to the customers has been for nothing.

> Tip: Always get commitment to your project from the entire board of directors in writing before starting, otherwise you may find that you have wasted months of your time.

It is easy to undervalue design and developments. If you set up a unique tailored supply chain in advance, ready to sustain quality, consistency, ethics and a good production price in the future, you won't have to go back to the drawing board again and again. Designing and sourcing is a process of a minimum of four to six months, even when you know what you are doing.

Here are a few pointers to consider when you're looking for a factory to manufacture your products:

- What do you know about the factory?
- Is it ethical? Are they part of any certification bodies?
- Are the workers cared for?
- Is it a practising family business? (if that's important to you)
- Which other companies does it manufacture for?
- Have you asked those companies for their opinions of the factory?
- Have you tested the quality of the end product?
- Can people at the factory all translate technical drawings and designs competently?
- Have you checked the factory's testimonials from other clients?
- Can they source the kind of fabrics you want and need?

I personally visit every single factory I work with. Either I or one of my colleagues will carefully oversee every new production run to check everything is as we want it before we go to full production. When I work with a new mill, factory or maker, I test every stage of the system it offers, and most of all, I test their ability to understand, communicate and deliver what they say they will deliver, and whether they are on time. How else can I know for sure what's going on with the product and the people who make it? I understand that you are not likely to have the time to do as I do, which is why I wholeheartedly recommend working with an expert to help redesign your uniforms or products.

> Tip: If you start the design, re-development and implementation of a product all over again with a new supplier, it can take another nine months to a year. Think carefully about whether the cost of the transition, the volume commitment, the quality and the ethics of the new company are right for your brand.

Other risks of changing your supplier include:

- No control over the timing of the new sample developments
- A possibility that the new supplier won't provide a fitting service and accommodate the diversity of body shapes among your staff
- Production delays – it's common to have unworkable heat conditions and power cuts due to the weather in countries such as India and Bangladesh. The working conditions are notoriously low for workers, and factories in these countries tend to be used by the low price-point end of the fashion and workwear industry
- Quality control will need to be overseen by an in-house expert
- You will need off-the-shelf uniforms to cover the time delay caused by starting again from scratch, then later dispose of them
- Not as effective at resourcing
- Don't have as much loyalty from fabric suppliers

S: STYLE

Your uniform has to have it, and it must work for every body shape in a timeless fashion.

Whether it's colour, fabric or fit, a few little tweaks can make all the difference to what the garments your staff are wearing will portray for you. Even practical clothing can have style and taste. Establish the tone of your brand and decide how best to translate that tone into your textiles.

For example, a restaurant group wanted to add a quirky retro feel to its tables by using its brand colours on napkins and for contrast-colour aprons. This worked so well as a signature style in its flagship restaurant that the group duplicated the theme and changed the colours for all the restaurants, making them stand out and uniting them with textile touches. The staff loved being able to style them individually, by rolling the tops, using the reverse side of the apron, tying the belts multiple times round the front or tying them more times round the back; some had them low slung on their hips and others had them tied higher round the waist.

How people express themselves through their style fascinates me. I love people watching, especially in vibrant areas while they're scouring markets or second-hand shops. Everyone is unique, but some people know how to express their style and values better than others. Some people need a little help bringing their style out, and that comes with confidence.

If you have no idea what looks great on you or your staff, it's a problem. I suggest getting a stylist to help you with finding your best colours, shapes and personality styling. We all have so many situations in which we have to wear many hats and still look the part, so dressing in a versatile way helps when you need to switch roles.

For example, I'm a mum, a parent, a wife, a daughter, a sister, a fundraiser, a yogi, a health fanatic, a professional, a leader, a fashion designer, a style queen, a vintage lover and a friend. I dress for how I want to feel and what best suits my situation. Sometimes, I need to dress to make sure others feel they can know, like and trust me, both in my work and in my life. It is important to get this right. I have learned how to be me in every situation, wearing what I want to wear, while bringing out my best self and being fit for purpose and relevant.

Give this some thought and have fun with it. You need to invest in what works for you in multiple ways. Inspiration is all around you, so look at what clothing styles others like. If you see a style you admire, it is worth asking the wearer where they shop.

There are many stylists out there, so find one near you whom you can resonate with. They will help you address the dressing issues you have in certain situations. Some people know what to wear for work, but don't have a clue what suits them casually, and vice versa.

When I consulted a professional stylist, I discovered I have an autumn colouring, and the clothes I wear needed to have yellow tones in them. My personality style is Princess Adventurer, which means I like to be facing a challenge or striding through the great outdoors, so I wear trousers a lot. That certainly makes sense – I once hired a scooter in Hung To, Vietnam, and set off into the rural areas with no map. At the same time, I need to look glamorous and have a bit of sparkle, so I always wear jewellery and make sure I'm coordinated even if I'm in jogging bottoms, they need to match the top and the trainers etc.

Find out your style code and embrace it. See how it works in every area of your life, and notice the difference in how you look and feel. In the case of your business or brand, how do you want it to make people feel? What three words would you use to sum up your personal brand? For example, I'm magnetically resourceful and courageous. Take those three words and embed them into your brand's visual language expressions.

Ask style questions of your brand or your personal brand look. Is it formal, casual, glamorous, sporty, relaxed, comfortable, quirky, modern, minimalistic, traditional, retro, or a combination of a few of those ideas? Do you have a hierarchy of staff? Do the styles of the uniforms need to show ranking and authority? You want to make sure the uniforms accommodate the practical features of each job role, but also make staff members feel fabulous in what they are wearing. They should feel confident and empowered while meeting and greeting all levels of customers and colleagues.

Let's take an example. A client wanted their staff's day and evening uniforms to be clothes they could feel comfortable, attractive and proud to be seen in, even if they were carrying out cleaning duties.

The duties of the staff were varied. They could be cleaning, doing the laundry, organising rooms, making beds, prepping canapés or doing cloakroom duties, setting out grand halls or greeting guests. On top of this, they could expect to cross paths with staff from different departments who didn't wear uniforms, and greet the special guests as they arrived, taking care of their domestic needs for the duration of their stay.

At the time, the client's staff felt very self-conscious in what they had to wear. The uniform had not changed for over thirty years, so it had become dated and out of style. It also wasn't serving them on the comfort front.

The task was to design a dress and jacket or cardigan so the staff could easily switch between behind-the-scenes and front-of-house roles, and always look and feel their best. The staff were all ladies of various shapes, ranging from size 6 to size 26. Somehow, my team and I needed to make them all look and feel good.

First of all, we switched the colour of the dresses from white to navy. We also combined two dresses into one, so they had one navy dress. Navy is a far more flattering and universal colour than white, and it looks good on all skin types. We then looked at traditional shapes with a princess line (cut in long panels without a separating seam at the waist) that would flatter and flare. We also looked at an elbow-length sleeve. A gusseted neckline added a contrast edging that was stunning and would flatter a large bust or add shape to a smaller chest.

One of the fundamentals was the dress length (to the hem). We decided that below the knee would look attractive on all the ladies' body shapes while concealing any insecurities some wearers might have about their legs or knees. Another key to the success of the dress was to offer options on the back length, as this transforms the fit. Where the shaping of the waist and hips on a garment sits on a person's body is dependent on the back length. I discovered when I was young that I have a short back length which means that clothes often gape at the back of my waist and won't sit right on my hips.

We suggested three back lengths of short (14.5–15.5 inches), regular (16–17 inches) and long (17.5–18 inches) so that all body proportions were flattered and hit the waist and the hips of all three types of body lengths. The result was clothing that looked made to measure, yet it was a simple pattern tweak that could be graded into the master fit set of patterns, then this could be scaled for bulk even though it was a bespoke fit that we had designed from the beginning.

P: PEOPLE

People are everything to me. I love them with a passion. It's what I love about hospitality – people are the heart of every organisation that I work with.

My team and I choose very carefully which suppliers we work with so that we can have great quality relationships, which makes whatever we are doing much more fun and meaningful. Our suppliers are king; they are so special to us. Every supplier we have worked with and continue to work with is a family business. Most people only focus on the client, who is hugely important and we know we go the extra mile for our clients, that's why they stay with us for so long, but a lot of people forget that the supplier is also hugely important too. It is important to me to work together to keep these kinds of businesses afloat and thriving.

Surround yourself with the best people and value them. When you look after somebody, they naturally want to look after you. It creates a symbiotic relationship, and together you do so much more. Find your tribe, test their values are a match for yours, and the product they provide will be as good as the people – as long as you communicate clearly and honestly with them your relationships will always go the mile and last as long as a lifetime.

For your team and talents, seek to bring the best out in people around you by being the best you possibly can be – having high integrity, authenticity and honesty in your personal and professional life. Help people shine. If you need more clarity on this I highly recommend doing the Landmark Forum run by Landmark Education. With our clients, we want them to look their best so that they are expressing themselves through their textiles in a way that they wish to be perceived. If someone told you what to wear each day, would you not want it to feel right for you and your role? A good uniform can dramatically affect your staff's energy, unity and sense of belonging. That is how vital it is to igniting a team and environment.

O: ORGANISATION

It may sound obvious, but I'll say it anyway – you need to record each step, process and technical detail while you're designing your new uniform, so you have a finished product template ready to take to your factory. Sometimes you can find factories that document everything thoroughly for you once you start working with them, but before you get to that point, you need to be able to communicate what you want clearly.

Work out all your timings backwards. I have designed a six-step programme that helps you to ensure your product journey is organised and structured. We will cover the six-step process in more detail in Chapter Six.

K: KINDNESS AND KARMA

Being kind and caring with everyone you partner with or serve is a basic requirement. If you communicate clearly and politely to help everything run smoothly, you will likely get a seamless ecosystem of you serving clients and factories serving you.

I recently spoke to a representative at one of my British factories about respect, and she replied, 'If only everyone thought like you.' When I asked what she meant, she said that she had spoken to several companies that had started working with the factory. Many of these companies' representatives had said the way to get the best out of their suppliers was to speak to them harshly and with little respect.

I believe you have to treat all relationships like precious jewels. Yes, there is time to be tough and lay down the law, agreeing deadlines and boundaries, but people will stick with you if you're kind, straight and loyal to them. It's a partnership, whether you're sourcing from overseas or in this country. No one will want to do much for you if you are rude or disrespectful.

Once or twice now, I have dealt with unscrupulous individuals who had no qualms about saying one thing and doing another. Kindness is also about integrity. If you break your word, you break trust. Being kind and considerate does work, but do follow your instincts to make sure no one takes your kindness for granted.

You can't buy loyalty and authenticity in relationships; it has to be earnt and built. What comes around goes around. Kindness creates karma.

E: ENDLESS SUSTAINABLE SUPPLY

When you start sampling and sourcing a product, you need to think about whether you will be able to duplicate it and repeatedly order it. Is the supply sustainable from the tailor or manufacturer at the cost and quality you require?

There is no point making up a sample or sourcing materials if you can't get them again. You need to know that you can scale up or repeat what you're doing easily and ethically in manageable, affordable volumes so that you can fully calculate the cost from the beginning.

A sustainable, seamless and repeatable supply chain is key to manufacturing your products again and again. It needs to be a long-term system-based solution to get the best value return for your invested time and money, so make sure it's future proof.

SUMMARY

The BESPOKE™ principles are essential to keep in mind when you're sourcing fabrics, textiles and products that reflect you brand values.

To recap, BESPOKE™ stands for:

- Beauty
- Ethics
- Style
- People
- Organisation
- Kindness and karma
- Endless sustainable supply

If you apply these principles to all your projects, whether in your business or in your life in general, you won't go far wrong and you will have created something beautiful and BESPOKE™.

CHAPTER SIX /

The Six-step

Process

6.1 – Bespoke Textiles 6 step process.

Whether you're creating a uniform to reflect your brand or building a product range, it is often difficult to know where to begin. My favourite place to start is to draw on what I am inspired by, identifying my needs and desires.

What is your goal? What outcome do you wish to achieve? Is it a perfect uniform or a capsule collection of wardrobe essentials that you can scale to fit and look good on both small and large bodies? Is it an interiors collection? It's all about being clever and designing to the individual's

109

practical needs while making sure your design can work in a mass market as well as being long lasting.

6.2 – Crochet and appliqué design illustration.

In this chapter, I will talk you through the six step process that your product will go through. The steps are:

- Discover
- Design
- Develop
- Produce
- Quality control
- Deliver

Let's now look at each step in detail.

STEP 1: DISCOVER

This is where you begin the journey to design your perfect uniform or product. Look at your brand style. What is the purpose of the product? What are the garment requirements? How many will you need and by when? What type of style, trims, and details inspire you? What is currently working? Or what's not working and needs changing?

I begin by gathering together all my ideas and influences, which sometimes means using things I have kept for twenty years. I have in my archives collections of old samples I bought in markets in Hong Kong, India, Bali, Thailand, Vietnam, and all over Europe.

In the UK, I especially love charity and vintage shops as you already know! As well as the pop-up markets of Brixton and Shoreditch – and I also love the vintage shop Rokit. In London, there are inspiring places everywhere if you don't mind seeking them out, including the iconic Portobello Market where new things arrive every week. I look for interesting, simple, classic shapes: a brooch; an old cardigan; a detail on a shoe. Keep a treasure chest of things that you love and are inspired by, and maybe you can redesign, adapt or remake them to use as the basis for your product sample.

Raincoat Design

6.3 – The recycled raincoat concept development board.

Of course, you can gather ideas and research on the internet, creating a Pinterest board, but the old-fashioned and fun way is to create a mood board by tearing pages from magazines. Create a research folder or stick pictures and fabric samples into a sketch book or on to an A1/A2 pin board. Get inspired and have fun. You can refine the ideas later.

STEP 2: DESIGN

It all starts with a sketch or design template. Build up your designs either by drawing them yourself or by getting a designer to do it for you. Make sure you have plenty to choose from and then whittle the number down. Much will depend on the quality of the designer you have chosen: you will need to establish how good they are at translating your ideas and look for somebody else if they are not good enough. You will know what you want as soon as you see it, so keep going until you find something you love.

Your design will never be mediocre if you really explore what you want and get it made especially for you. Your initial designs may be classic, simple, clever or elegant, and then when you've found one you're happy with, you can add the bespoke touches that will connect it to your brand.

I remember reading an article about the famous product designer Philippe Starck, now known more for his iconic interior design than anything else, and how he would work at his desk and sketch, sketch, sketch. He had a cupboard by the side of him with fifteen drawers, and he would put all his initial ideas into the top drawer. Next, he would look through them, editing them, keeping only those he felt were interesting, and putting them into the second drawer down. Then he would refine these interesting ideas further by moving the stand-out sketches to the next drawer down, and so on. As the ideas/sketches went further down the hierarchy of drawers, they got closer and closer to the perfect idea, and whatever ended up in the bottom drawer was a winner. Starck knew it was something he had to produce because it had stayed at the top of the pile after fifteen edits.

It's the same with the sketches, magazine scraps and samples you collect together on your mood board. When you hang on to something long enough, either it means something to you or there is something you need to do with that idea, but you don't know what yet. Discovering your or your brand's style is all about deciding, defining, eliminating and consolidating your design, then creating a prototype.

If you want to find a freelance designer to help you with this process, I would recommend either going to a university such as the London College of Fashion or browsing websites like www.fashionworkie.com or www.peopleperhour.com. Alternatively, there is an agency that supports design and manufacture called Fashion

Angel, which has fantastic members' resources. Be inspired by other start-up product/garment businesses, go to their seminars, have one to ones, download information packs from their websites, etc. Alternatively, you could use your Facebook and LinkedIn networks to put the word out there that you're in need of a designer's services.

I personally love a website called Fiverr where I can get anything designed or created. It can be hit and miss, so success depends on how well I communicate my ideas at the beginning.

Providing style examples of what you want, and a clear explanation, means you will spend less time tweaking your idea. If you make a few mistakes, not to worry – that's part of the process, and sometimes those mistakes will reveal a better direction for you to go in. Allow yourself lots of time to get it right.

STEP 3: DEVELOP

The developmental stage is where you take your technical measurements, details, trims and fabric references, sample ideas and components, and put them into a tech pack. Once you have your tech pack ready, select a good source for materials and a factory that will be sustainable for resupply, then create and test your pattern. Allocate it a style number, then pass your tech pack to your factory to make the first prototype sample and get a costing. You may need to remake samples two to three times before you're happy with the finished product.

Let's cover all of that in detail.

This step can be time consuming to get right. Once you have a strong design that you want to get prototyped, you will need to get the technical specifications drafted, which includes a technical drawing and details all the necessary information. Your spec will be more evolved and you'll avoid mistakes in the making of the product if you have every measurement, material, print positioning, stitch type, label requirement, trim, button size, zip/fastening method, colour and Pantone number included in the technical specification. You then have what I referred to in the first paragraph as a tech pack.

You can refine your design and select the one you want to make. You may need to refine your designs two to three times, scaling them up to see how they work in different sizes, which will take three to six months. During this process, you can test factories that will fit your brief, make your product come to life and perfect it.

To be able to communicate your requirements to your suppliers/factories clearly, ask yourself the following questions:

- How many units do I want to make of one item?
- When do I want them by? (Set yourself a realistic timescale)
- What kind of fabrics or materials am I looking to have the item made in?
- Do I need the suppliers/factories to source the fabrics?
- When you're looking at potential factories, ask their representatives:
    - Who else do you work for?
    - Are you operating at my market level?
    - Are you accredited?
    - What's your speciality?

Google is an amazing resource to use to find anything from fabrics to factories, but it's not always clear whom you can trust. It can seem like a minefield of sampling while you try out different factories, but if you test, test, test, it will become clear.

If your product is going to be something that involves a large volume order made of silk or cotton, then I would certainly suggest you consider testing and comparing Asian factories. Make sure you have multiple supply sources in case your first choice doesn't work out. Supply sources in Asia (mainly in Hong Kong, China, India, Sri Lanka, Vietnam and Indonesia) can make everything from scratch, including the fabric, so your design can be completely bespoke, but you can also take some things off the shelf or find some things in local markets. Don't reinvent the wheel if you don't have to: it's all about finding a way to provide a sustainable repeat supply chain for your product. Usually the further afield you work, the more detailed your technical information and visuals need to be.

You can have your product manufactured in Europe as well, but if you are using a material such as silk, it will involve a higher minimum order quantity and price point as the silk will have to be imported through a European wholesaler or agent. Silk is predominantly produced in China. If I'm working with a certain material I try to use the manufacturer closest to where the fabric is. If you are having it woven, or just buying it in ready made, this can make sense, as it saves money on raw material and importing costs or added margins from buying through an agent. Similarly, cotton or linen is produced in India, Pakistan and Turkey, so work with factories in those countries. However, if you initially want the flexibility of placing small orders that use fewer than 50 metres of fabric, then inland UK or European manufacturing will suit you better. If you're starting small, stay closer to home.

When you're deciding on the fabrics and materials for your product, where do you start? It's best to start in fabric retail shops and discover what you like and its contents and components, for example, 97% viscose and 3% spandex woven crepe. If you are in London, Berwick Street covers a large range of options. It is important to feel fabrics and see if you and your client like them, and also see how they hang, drape and stretch.

Once you've identified what you like, you can buy your prototype materials from the retailers. However, for production and costing your samples for scaling an order, I recommend you source a wholesale supplier online or at a trade fair such as the Textile Forum or Premier Vision. A wholesaler can provide the same or similar fabrics to the ones you have sourced from fabric retail shops.

If you are a more experienced buyer, or you require larger volumes of fabric (1,000 metres or more), source a mill. This will be the best and most cost-effective option for producing materials, and you will be able to ensure that every element of the fabric matches your performance requirements: for example, you could request that spandex and polyester be added to cotton or silk for better durability or price, ,or identify a texture ideal for being dyed and woven to your bespoke colour, design and weight. Or you might even want to specify the type of weave, for example, you could have a beautiful jacquard design woven into the cloth.

Once you have sent the supplier/factory a sketch, and simplified your information using clear diagrams, images of exact stitch details and a technical specification of the prototype, you can engage the factory to make your first sample. If your factory is overseas, expect a minimum of four weeks for your first prototype to be made and couriered back to you. If your factory is in the UK you may get it in less than two weeks, provided you can gather all the materials you need to have it made at the factory. For example, if we give our apron factory a brief it is a simple exercise for them, because we have a standard selection of stock fabrics. They can have a sample made in a week, which is great for our clients. So, simpler products with fewer sourcing needs are ideal for UK factories. Most factories will have their own courier, but they may choose to use yours, so make sure you have an account set up (as I'm sure most businesses already have) with one that you've tested and you know will give you the right service at the price you want. I use a lovely local family-based courier company that delivers locally, but they also have offices in Hong Kong and China that handle my overseas goods.

Your factory may need to source fabrics before making the actual sample. The first sample may not be in the exact fabric you want, but in a fabric that's similar. This stage is essential to see how the factory has interpreted your design. Look at the quality, the way the factory has handled and made the sample, the attention to detail and the finishing both on the inside and the outside. Ask yourself if they have understood your market aesthetic. It is really important to know whether they will be able to translate your technical specifications so as to get the best possible quality for the product price point. You want to be impressed rather than underwhelmed. This will also test whether there are massive gaps in the information that you have supplied and you need to fill in the blanks, and whether they are the right fit for this product. Go over the details yet again, and if you find your instructions contain all the specifications they need to contain, yet the product is still not right, you probably need to look for another supplier.

6.4 – Blanket swatches and label placement.

This is why I always like to test my products with at least two suppliers that I know, like and trust. After testing, one will become a clear leader you can work with, or perhaps a spare that you can fall back on. This is what we did when we were testing a new jacquard tie weave with two new factories in an artisan area of Northern China that could do good small minimums working at designer to mid-market level. They were both given the same Pantone number: one got the colour right but not the placement, the other got the placement right but not the colour. We knew the first factory could correct the placement, and it had made a supreme effort to get its samples to us on time. (The project had a tight timetable.) This made it easy to choose one supplier we could work with straight away, yet we still knew that the other, with some guidance, could work for us as a back-up. You definitely need to think about the easiest route to manufacture, and sometimes creating a product with the minimum of production headaches means paying a little bit more.

Once you are happy with your sample, you can start refining it. If you can't find the exact fabric you want to use in your end product, you may need to develop the blend, yarns, colours, weave construction and weight of the fabric yourself, which can sometimes take as long as the sample stage. To be on the safe side, allow yourself one year to design, source, develop and deliver the products.

Trust between you and all the suppliers in your supply chain is essential, but there should also be mutual trust with the client. Co-creating a new product for them may entail changes as you evolve your ideas. If it's a good project, you should be able to build a very close relationship with them, based on the depth of knowledge and expertise you both develop when working collaboratively. Often, you just know when you can trust a person or company; with very little information, you can feel know this is the right direction to go in. That is the time to take a semi-risk to explore the relationship further.

As things evolve, look at how they are panning out with your suppliers to gain insights as to whether to continue to work with them. Taking risks can give you scrapes, but they are essential to growing your business and yourself. If your instincts are telling you to change sources or direction to protect your integrity, brand and product, don't ignore them, otherwise your sanity could suffer. Believe me, I've been in many a situation where I've had to disentangle myself from a partnership rather quickly to minimise the damage.

Years ago, I was involved in a collaboration. My part in the collaboration was to work on the garment design, shape and fit, sourcing and production. The fabric was to be made from recycled water bottles, which was new sourcing territory for me.

Around the same time, I was introduced to an overseas agent who was supposedly an expert in eco sourcing.

Thinking they would know more than I did about this area, and based on a recommendation from someone I trusted, I decided to work with this agent.

On email and on paper, the partnership appeared to be working well. Then I flew to visit the agent to get the nitty gritty of the project set up for production. My husband and I had a six-month-old baby at the time, so I took my entire family – the baby, our two-year-old, and my husband – with me as I was still breast feeding. My husband would then be able to look after the children during the day while I was meeting with the agent. It was also a wonderful opportunity to treat my family to an adventure in a different country.

I arrived at the offices of my new partner. It is weird sometimes when I think I know what someone is going to look like, and then they turn out to be different in every way when I meet them. When I met my new partner, my first feelings were shock and discomfort. They were the complete opposite of what I had been expecting. There was none of the warm, honest aura that I had been hoping for.

My instinct kicked in to tell me something wasn't right with this partnership, but as I had flown all the way to my partner's country, I decided to carry on and visit the factory they were proposing to use. We'd planned the costings, margins, volumes and commissions over email, the design was all complete and almost ready for production, so I wasn't expecting any surprises.

When meeting with the factory at their offices, I suddenly found they couldn't do the 1,000 pieces we had planned. It would have to be nearer to 3,000 pieces because of the minimum order requirement of the special base cloth made from recycled water bottles. This was quite a concern as I had thought we had everything all planned, and we needed to meet the client's target price.

The agent I had chosen to start working with, who was introducing me to this factory, suggested I call the client to see if I could get them to increase to 3,000 instead of 1,000 units or to ask me to source another fabric supplier and cost. The client was happy to up the volume, but I wasn't happy with the unexpected change to the minimum order number and price.

The last straw for me was when the agent (the new partner I was collaborating with) sent emails behind my back to the client. We had had full transparency between each other but suddenly they started doing the dirty. The client found these emails so derogatory that they sent them on to me, and I was shocked. How could I trust a partner who was trying to undermine my relationship with my client? And when the production material came in, we discovered two things: the waterproof coating wasn't waterproof, and the fabric had fake certification and wasn't made from recycled water bottles at all.

Luckily, going back to my principles of working with people you know, like and trust I had developed a relationship with another great designer and excellent sourcing partner. He was brilliant and went straight to the best green fibres mill in Taiwan on my behalf. He got the authentic fabric, certification and all the information we needed to move the production on and rectify the project as quickly as possible.

> Tip: Trust your instincts from the beginning of a partnership, before things go too far and you have wasted resources, time and money.

Ten years later, another trust issue rose up with another potential new partner. Having learned from my last experience, I was able to sense things weren't right and change the factory as early as possible to serve the client smoothly and avoid problems. My instinct was mainly triggered by the partner's reluctance to sign a non-disclosure agreement (to protect me from a repeat of my previous experience). After I had been chasing them to sign it for two months, they suddenly came up with different terms that would not have benefited me.

I also sensed that they had a trust issue as they did not want me to keep a sample they had sent to me at my studio. I trusted the concerned feeling in my gut that was telling me that once monetary exchanges became involved in our partnership, things could only get worse. I was not willing to take any risks with my business, or with my new client who meant a huge amount to me.

> Tip: Don't do anything without signing terms on both sides. I would also recommend signing a non-disclosure agreement before you do business with a new partner. Definitely don't test a new relationship on a very important project. My old boss Colin, from English Eccentrics, said to me recently that it's a question of making sure everyone is bringing the same amount to the table and gain in equal proportions from the collaboration that keeps the relationship balanced. You need to be sure that you can trust a partner to act in your best interests.

When you are looking to partner with someone at the developmental stage of your project, ask to see examples of their work in the form of samples and products. Some questions you could ask yourself are:

- How willing are they to assist me?
- Do they have any references from people they have worked with?
- What information do they need to make a prototype?
- How long have they been in business?
- How protected are my designs?
- Do we get on?
- What can they bring to the table that you can't provide?
- What can you bring to the table that they can't provide?
- Can you get feedback on them from previous partners or even from their clients before committing yourself?

This will give you a feel for how knowledgeable and suitable for the project they are.

I learned from Dan Priestley when I did the Key Person of Influence course that when partnering you need to keep ownership of two corners of the triangle: the product, the brand or the distribution. In fact, you need to own at least one of the three or you will lose control. In my case, suddenly the balance tipped and I was not going to own the copyright of the designs, or rights to the relationship, which meant in turn losing the value I'd worked so hard to build. Keep any partnership balanced and working for you.

A good relationship should be based on honesty, your partner giving you as much as you give them. I like to build relationships up before I do anything together with a partner. My motto is: 'You can't ask a favour from a stranger, but my lesson has always been to get it in writing early on.'

6.5 – Use the Zappar app to scan the code and watch the video of me explaining how we developed the recycled raincoat 10 years ago.
https://www.youtube.com/watch?v=dMNl43T2P2O

STEP 4: PRODUCE

When you have approved your pre-production sample and price, and your tech packs and pattern grades are all compiled, confirm lead times and you're ready to roll.

You usually need to put a deposit of between 30% and 50% down with the factory to proceed with production, so if you're making your product for orders or on a client's behalf, be sure to get a deposit from the client before you start. This will cover your production costs, so should anything go wrong (which it rarely does), you're covered.

The balance will then be your gross profit – if you've calculated your costings well enough to ensure a good margin.

To prepare your product for bulk production, make a master pattern for it. In some cases, the factory will be able to do this for you, or you could employ a freelance pattern cutter. It all depends on how tricky the shape is and whether you want to perfect that before sending your ideas on to a factory to prototype.

Occasionally, your pre-production sample may not be produced in the correct colour, possibly because the fabric needs to be dyed to match your chosen colour. As long as the quality of the fabric is correct, you can see how it will drape, which is the most important aspect to get right at this stage. Remember to get a fabric swatch in the final colour, and to approve the colour and any other changes with your supplier before continuing with production.

In most cases, the factory can make a full pattern with grades. Nowadays, the factory pattern cutter can work from the master pattern you provide, or they can tweak and amend the pattern as needed before the full grading. I always then get a full sized set of pre-production samples made. In fashion, we generally work from sizes 8 to 18, or small to extra large in casual clothing. However, with the growing diversity in size of the population, clients' orders can range from size 6 to size 26 for ladies.

The standard grading rule for scaling your sizes is 4 cm around the body width, the collar and length grades being in proportion. Generally, your approved sample is in size 10 or small, or, for men, a size 38, the reason being that a standard tailor's dummy is a size 10. I use a Kennett and Lindsell; they are the best couture stand for the whole fashion and clothing industry. Grading is applied to scale the sizing down to 6 or 8/extra small, or size 36 for men, and graded up to size 12/medium, or 40 for men, depending on what your staff's/client's sizing requirements are.

The pattern cutter at the factory can put all this together to create sets of master blocks for your pattern per style ready for your repeat orders in the future. If you want to control your patterns and fit samples more in-house, then I recommend employing a freelance pattern cutter. Ask around or search the internet for someone local to you. As with all services you use, find out who else they work with and ask for references. You can communicate with your own pattern cutter directly to make a perfect prototype and toile (sample) quickly and accurately before sending it off to your factory. This is a more expensive option in the short term but will save time and possibly money in the long run.

By this stage, you should know what fabric you are using, what the development costs of the sample are, if there are any extra pattern costs, what the courier charges are, and have a quote for the finished item in production. These are your setup costs, and they are a one-off.

You also need to think about whether you require any tagging. If the answer is yes, will you be supplying it or will you be sending artwork to the factory to have tags printed for you? Even more importantly, where would you like the tags to be attached? Certain garments can be ruined by incorrect tagging. If you haven't already confirmed the details of where you would like your tags attached, this is your last chance to do so.

Designing, developing, sourcing, and compiling all the technical information for your factory can cost between £250–£2,000, depending on the complexity of your project and how many styles it entails: this is the cost for about three good styles. It also depends on how readily available materials and construction requirements are. Also, factor in whether you are sourcing inland or overseas, and if any factory visits are required. Shipping, importing and duty costs all need to be added. The biggest cost in design development is the research and sourcing time you need to gather information for a rich supply base, then compile this information to create your unique garments, samples and fit prototypes. I once made seventeen samples for one client to test all the sizes and try out the different fit features they needed. It was just for one man's and one woman's shirt, but it's amazing how many 'retweaks' you can do before you get to the final perfect sample.

Here is a budgeting guide for designing and developing your products:

Budget

Designing	£100–£1,000
Pattern	£80–£450 (approximately)
Toile/prototype	£50–£300

You may need to do two to three samples before the final fit/fabric sample can become your 'sealed sample' (as it's known in the trade. Sealed means seal of approval or gold seal) for production.

Specification sheet/tech pack	£50–£300
Grading	£50–£250 approximately
Total set up costs per style	£530–£2,300

Planning production costs using an example of shirts:

Fabric per garment:	£5.50
CMT (cut, make and trim)	£12

(If you're using a factory in the Far East, it can source your trims, for example, buttons, zips, bindings, interlinings, to your requirements, so you will either get a price for fabric, or for CMT only, without fabric.)

Delivery approximately 10%	£1.75
Total:	£18.75 per garment in production

If your production is in China or India, add duty of 9–12% to the cost price of each item, minus £2.10 (eg, £5.50 + £12.00 = £17.50 x12%). Total with duty = £20.85 per garment in production. The import VAT on cost price is 20%, minus £3.50 (you can claim VAT back, if you are VAT registered, against your sales VAT).

The cost for CMT would be agreed depending on the volume you are making. This works as a sliding scale:

- 100 items @ £12
- 500 items @ £11
- 1,000 items @ £10

Don't forget to factor in your reordering ratios, which may be of lower volume if you are just topping up the core stock, so you need to know the cost of the minimum reorder. As you grow more successful those reorder volumes may increase and the price can drop down again, but in some scenarios the price has to go up.

It's always in your favour to order as many items as you can, as long as you know you can sell them. Test that there is a market out there for your product, especially if price is key to your budget or business model. Do not fall into the trap of optimism and over-order on stock. Your products need strong marketing strategies behind them to support the sales.

However, if your product is a uniform for your staff or items for your interiors that will need replenishing constantly, the advice is the opposite: make sure you never run out of stock. Have a stock level that will cover you until you can get a minimum reorder made up. Factor in a lead time so you can order your product well in advance of when you need it. The lead time can vary, from a minimum of four weeks if the items are made in the UK and the material is already in stock, right through to sixteen weeks if you have to start from scratch, having the fabric woven as well.

SIZE	EXTRA SMALL		SMALL		MEDIUM		LARGE	
UK	4-6		8-10		12-14		16-18	
US	2-4		6-8		10-12		14-16	
EURO	32-34		36-38		40-42		44-46	
	INCH	CM	INCH	CM	INCH	CM	INCH	CM
BUST	32½-33½	82-85	34½-35½	88-90	37-38½	94-98	40-42	102-107
WAIST	24½-25½	62-65	26½-27½	67-70	29-30½	75-77	32-34	81-86
HIP	35-36	89-91	37-38	94-97	39½-41	100-104	42½-44½	108-113

6.6 – Sizing Chart.
These charts should be used as a general fitting guide only.
Size available and individual sizing may vary by style.

6.7 – Use the Zappar app to scan the code and watch the video on the factory
floor, showing how shirts are sewn together with specialist machinery.
https://youtu.be/AzvsKjjVekQ

Your order needs to be based on factual projections that will tide you over for at least six months. In hospitality, you need 30%–50% surplus stock of uniforms in all sizes to cover a 50%–300% turnover rate annually. Be prepared to review stock levels after one, two and three months so you can be ready to reorder ahead of time.

What you can guarantee is that your most popular items will be sizes small and medium (sizes 10–14) for women, and sizes medium and large for men, so double up on your order in these popular sizes.

Now you are armed and ready with your costings, budget plans, pattern samples and technical packs, and fabrics (which may or may not be ordered by the factory on your behalf), but no process runs smoothly without people you can trust and rely on, and vice versa. The people you work with need to have a system in place to be reliable. Make it a priority to get to know how they work, what they do best, and what they need from you to make the project run smoothly.

Your factory will now give you a production timeline (if it hasn't already). This is a plan of all the stages, from receipt of the deposit through to the delivery. If you're short of time, you may need to get your goods delivered by courier. Otherwise, if your goods are coming from overseas, they can be shipped.

It usually takes four weeks for your factory to make your order. The order is complete once the weaving, dying, trim sourcing, making and pattern marking are all finished, which can take between four to six weeks to pre-prepare. Many factories, if they are smart, are already lining things up in the background to go straight into production, which could make it a short four weeks for you. Otherwise it could be four to six weeks on top of the four weeks, making eight to ten weeks in total from start to finish, from making the fabric trims through to finishing the final product, including quality control.

I love how factories lay out their production: they dedicate certain lines according to particular items: for example, if a shirt is being made one person is responsible just for side seams, one just for collars, the next person is responsible just for sleeves and so on. The shirt is passed down until it reaches the end of the production line. So, if you have a large production of 10,000 pieces, the entire factory could be working on your one or two shirts. If you have a small production, the factory may only have one line dedicated to it and be working on other garments, but the production will be of a similar structure. Once it is complete, the product moves on to the quality control stage, where all the stress points that we have earmarked are checked one by one. Many factories know these elements inside out and will check completely against the 'production seal sample', which is what you want. Then the first shipment samples will be packed and sent off to you, ready for you to inspect yourself, to approve that the production is absolutely going to plan and is a perfect match with the original sample.

> Tip: I recommend that you, or a representative from your team or an experienced agent, visit the factory in person so you can be sure to work through and resolve any issues quickly and confirm that everything is right, not only for your peace of mind but also for your client's. You need to know that the factory is maintaining the integrity of your product, brand and business.

The cutting and lay plans aim to achieve the most economical use of the fabric. Often, this this will all be done in bulk: layers of fabric are stacked up and cut with a hand blade. This is not usually possible with refined fabric like chiffon, so each layer has to be cut separately. This makes it much more expensive (hence the cost of couture) but the factory will know what's most required and set a cost according to what's most appropriate for your production and fabric. I first saw this process when I was eighteen, doing work placement in a wetsuit factory in Cornwall, and it is fascinating to watch. The neoprene used in the wetsuits was so thick, the fabric layers were half a metre high.

Sometimes the fabric has a few flaws and the cutters have to cut round them by hand, which can delay the production start date by a few days. It can also alter the quantity that you planned on ordering. I always tell clients to expect 3%–5% of the bulk volume in extra or fewer units to act as a tolerance percentage, as most factories order 10% more fabric than they will need to allow for any faults. Even machines can't be perfect when they're weaving, and there may be manual errors from the factory workers. I always have respect and admiration for the great work that the factory does in pulling all of the processes together: creating, making, trimming, finishing, pressing, checking, packing, tagging, and counting before finally delivering the product to your door.

My favourite stage of the process is when I see my creation being put together into an end product. It's a proud moment. If I can, I always visit the factory for the first stages of production, especially for new or complicated items or with a new factory, to see the procedures and speak to the workers. I find it thrilling to get hands on, and I realise there can still be minor errors that need to be tweaked or nipped in the bud right at the beginning of production.

STEP 5: QUALITY CONTROL

I have people I can trust and I know the quality standards in the factories I use. It's all about the standards you want to set, and you need to understand these yourself to check that they are being maintained satisfactorily by others. If it's your first production, you either need to inspect the factory yourself or insist on seeing shipment samples of the first run of production. If there is a problem, immediately ask the factory to stop production and send further samples. Once you are satisfied that everything is correct with your pre-production sample, the factory can proceed and update the lead time if necessary.

This is one of the most important checks you need to do before your product is delivered. Be smart. If you are not an expert in this area, then employ someone who is. Things can go horribly wrong if you are not used to managing the production and quality control process and if you don't yet have enough experience with working with the factory in question to know whether their consistent quality is a match to your expectations. You want to win by getting it right the first time around, as the cost of losing can be huge. Once you have found an expert you trust, make sure you listen to and act on their advice. They are experts for a reason.

> Tip: Don't get in the way of the expert when it isn't your area of expertise.

There are some simple products like aprons or napkins that can be approved at the pre-production sample stage or via a photo.

The same is true if you know your suppliers well and have used them to make these items before. It depends on your experience and the strength of your relationship and trust.

When garments are more complex, there's more to go wrong, so then I like to check that everything is correct all through the production. I request a set of all the graded samples, called shipment samples, in all sizes. The competencies of a production line are very different to those of a sampling machinist/maker, and what can be made as a one-off item can be challenging to duplicate in large quantities. If you don't know what challenges you may need to meet, it is best to ask for a piece from production and check it yourself to put your mind at rest.

> Always request a pre-production sample (final approval sample) and a shipment sample from the first few items of bulk production.

Once I have my samples from production, I check the sizes, making sure that all the grades are to ratio. I then check the key measurements, the stitching, the trims, the finishing of hems, the weights of the interlinings, etc. If it's all good, I get in touch with the factory immediately to say I want to proceed.

On the odd occasion that there is a major problem and the factory needs to halt production, somebody needs to pay them a visit, get on a conference call, or get an agent who knows what they are doing and is well briefed to visit the factory to rectify the problem quickly. With the options of video calls and WhatsApp, there are many efficient ways to communicate with people around the world, and nowadays couriers are able to deliver to you within twenty-four hours from most countries. Everything can be sorted if you have trust, clear instructions, and a willingness to work it out together.

> Tip: Ask for close-up photos of key areas that are tricky to sew. If it has been done in a rush, the quality could have slipped, and without looking at the work before it leaves the factory, you won't know this until the product is delivered.

When you are liaising with your supplier on how your goods are to be packed, you may be offered a polyester bag, a cellophane bag, or, increasingly, tissue paper. Many clients now choose to go for no bags, to save waste. Which is fine as long as the goods are packed efficiently. Some clients request packs of ten or packs of two, just to reduce the number of bags, while being reassured that the goods are still covered for transit and storage. The factory representative will also ask if you have any specific printing instructions for the bags and how many pieces you want packed in a bag.

Clarify everything, right down to what information you would like on the boxes for shipping:

- Company name
- Purchase order number
- Style code
- Quantity per colour
- Site/destination (if applicable)

The factory can guide you if you are a first timer, but you need to be thinking about these details a month before shipping, if not right at the beginning of the production process, so the factory can prepare everything in advance. Keeping your production on track to the quality standards you require is key to delivery satisfaction. Then you can focus your energy on marketing, sales or the main core of your business, which in many cases for my clients is hospitality, and know the rest is taken care of.

STEP 6: DELIVERY

There are two options for the delivery of your goods: FOB (freight on board) or landed in the country of origin. If you choose landed, you will have to agree this with your factory in the price, and the factory representative will arrange delivery to your door. However, most factories use FOB, so you will need a shipper or import logistics company in your own country to handle the shipment transit and clearing at customs through to delivery to your destination.

There are so many companies available that can handle this process for you, so do a thorough Google search. Many have international networks that pick the shipment up in its country of export. I use Clearfast in Felixstowe: a friendly family-owned business that I can trust and speak to on the phone whenever I need an update.

Some factories will not release goods until the final payment is with them, which is why working with an experienced sourcing agent can be helpful. They will have much more negotiating power and knowledge than you if this is an unknown area for you.

The delivery methods will vary depending on whether the production is in Asia, America, Turkey, Europe or the UK. The country of manufacture, distance the shipment has to travel and the order quantity of your product will be the deciding factors as to whether you use sea freight, which involves a long shipping time, air freight, or courier. If the factory is in the UK or Europe, it is a simple courier job or lorry dispatch, and the products will be delivered to your door within two to seven days. This is a simple process which involves minimal paperwork. All you need is a packing list from the factory, and there should be no customs issues to deal with. Long-distance sea freight is standard but straightforward if you have a good shipping agent, though by far the most time consuming. Logistics partners can handle your paperwork, taking over from the factory once they've delivered it to the shipping port. They will then look after the goods while the freight is on board, and be responsible for them all the way through, from when they land at your port, via unloading, to customs clearance. Logistics partners will generate and handle all the relevant paperwork and the payments on your behalf. It is their insurance that covers the safety of your goods while in transit, but I have to say I have never ever had a problem with any goods, or any loss of goods, in the twenty years that I've been importing.

Your goods need to be delivered to the shipyard seven days before the cargo ship sails to be booked in and prepared for loading on to the container. From the moment the freight is on board, it will no longer be the factory's responsibility. If you are importing into the UK, the ports that it will generally come into will be Felixstowe or Southampton. If the goods are coming from China they will take twenty-two to thirty-five days to arrive at one of these ports. In addition, I would add seven days for clearing, unloading, customs and then delivery to your door.

If you don't have a history with a clearing agent or do not have a thirty-day terms account set up, you may need to pay VAT and duty costs before goods are released by customs. The paperwork your shipper will need to obtain from the factory before the shipment arrives is called the bill of lading. Your shipper won't be able to receive this paperwork until you have paid your factory, so it's a way of compelling you to complete payment but most of the time you will have paid your factory when the goods left their premises. Once you've demonstrated your brilliant ability always to pay on time the terms can be extended and the bill of lading can be handed over without delay. I'm sure you don't want to pay additional retention costs for storage at customs.

Here are some examples of lead times to add to production, depending on the country of manufacture of your goods:

- UK/Europe: seven days after the goods exit the factory
- Turkey: fourteen to twenty-one days, and you require lots of paperwork and a clearing agent
- USA, India and Asia: it can take between eighteen and thirty-five days, depending on the route of the ship, after the

goods exit the factory for them to be delivered to your door. You need to include a bill of lading and pay customs duty and VAT
· the bill of lading must be received to show to customs and to release goods

SUMMARY

There are a lot of practicalities to consider in the design, manufacture and delivery of your bespoke uniform or product, and we have covered them in detail in this chapter. If you follow this six-step procedure, applying the BESPOKE™ principles we covered in Chapter Five at each stage, you will find the whole process runs as smoothly as possible, leaving you free to concentrate on other areas of your business.

To recap, the six steps are:

· Discover
· Design
· Develop
· Produce
· Quality control
· Deliver

If you are unsure how best to proceed with any of these steps, there are a whole host of experts just waiting to help you out. Make sure you ask around to find someone you can really trust, and look at examples of their work and testimonials from former clients wherever you can. If you are looking to go into partnership with someone but feel that something isn't quite right, make sure you listen to your gut. The earlier you can get out of a bad partnership, the better.

I recommend a hands-on approach once you have found your ideal supplier, so you can make the most of the expertise of the supplier to come up with the best product for you. Even if it's not practical for you to visit the factory in person, make sure you either have a representative who can check the quality of their work or ask samples of your product at each stage of development along the way, so you can confirm that they are on the right track. Always request a pre-production sample and/or a shipment sample to approve before the rest of production continues.

If your goods have a long way to travel from their country of manufacture, make sure you work with a trusted logistics partner to take the stress out of overseeing safe shipment, from the moment your order is placed into the container to the moment it is delivered to you. They will also deal with customs and any payments that need to be made along the way.

With your finished product in your hands and your sustainable bespoke product supply chain set up, you will have completed your first journey into creating bespoke products or collections that will delight you, your staff and your customers. It's a proud moment. I hope you have learned a lot from the pages of this book and that I have inspired you to follow my advice to enhance the reputation of your brand. Most of all, I hope you will have fun.

Conclusion

I can hardly believe that I've reached the end of my exploration of the power of the textile touch, retracing my journey from discovering lost treasures in charity shops and using them to inform my own individual style, to founding a business based on my passion. Whether it's designing unique details for dresses for beautiful brands, enhancing the presentation of businesses, or dealing with orders both corporate and niche, it's work that is never less than absorbing and stimulating.

What matters is bringing textiles to life with my extensive knowledge of how garments are made and of how best to dress, of how to care – for the customer, for the fabrics and not least for the environment – and extending that to designing, developing and delivering products for thousands of people. If I were to distil what I have learned over the years about how to use textiles for maximum impact, these would be the key points:

- Everything should be made beautifully, and made to last.
- To design something well is to make it timelessly elegant, harnessing quality, style, and alignment with its purpose.
- A deep understanding of your client's unique values and needs is essential to be able to produce designs that resonate with their brand.

As an example of the timeless style qualities we Brits are known for, I would have to cite the Royal Family: their outstanding presentation and treasured traditions are an inspiration to the world. In the commercial arena, English Eccentrics are completely unique: they are bold with colour in a way that is unlike any other brand I've ever known, and their flair and imagination emerge more strikingly every time you look at one of their prints. This is because their designs have depth and meaning at their core. Helen David, who designed the prints, has drawn inspiration from all over the world: the scarf she created to commemorate women's contribution to the peace movement is on display at the Imperial War Museum, in London, to this day.

At the core of such iconic heritage brands are people with

great truth and integrity, people who care and who do things properly. They combine purpose with passion, style with rigour in a unique way, and it shows.

So I encourage you to go out, fully armed with ideas, processes and a mega to-do list, and make an impact with your vision, products, your stylish collections, or even your uniforms. Ensure they have longevity and leave a legacy – think heirlooms to be loved, used and treasured for several lifetimes.

Clothes and other beautiful things don't need to cost the earth; they can actually save it by being passed on and shared with future generations, who will love and cherish them just as we have. This approach honours the earth, the items, and their original owner. Such a truly circular economy reminds me of my grandmother's sewing box, which has lasted for generations and still sits in the centre of my studio. I drink my tea every morning from my 1953 Queen's Coronation mug, which also belonged to my grandmother. I take pleasure in this ritual every day (and I only ever wash the mug by hand, so it will last forever!).

I'm going to leave you with a quote I found in Helen Littman's (now Helen David) book of English Eccentrics prints. As I was searching for prints that we wanted to use again, I discovered this fantastic quote. It was written in the 1990s but is as relevant as if it had been written yesterday:

> 'As a reflection of the interest in recycling and keeping goods for longer, women in the 1990s are looking for a permanence in the goods that they buy. The craft aspect of merchandise is increasingly important. The idea is that things should be made to last.'

Helen David
English Eccentrics Prints

Acknowledgements

I'm so enormously proud and grateful to be able to bring this book into the world. It's the fruit of twenty-five years of experience, two intensive months of writing, and twelve months of tweaking and editing. As with all creations, the idea can arrive quite quickly, but the real magic happens in the development, and then in the giving birth.

I'd like to thank my family for being so supportive and patient while I was writing this book and building my business, putting up with all the early mornings, late nights, distractions, and multitasking it took to get it all done. You've been amazing at giving me the grace, the space, and the encouragement to persevere and to complete the things that I've always wanted to do. Thank you for allowing me to pull this body of work together, exploring the journey that's given me so much challenge, adventure, joy, and the ability to fulfil my dream of creating beautiful clothes and collections for myself and for others. I can now share this with others hungry to learn the same.

To my husband Nigel, who took the reins so willingly at home, especially during 2017, while I was building the next level of my business and writing this book at the same time: your belief in me has powered me on and you have been a constant rock in my life, giving me a foundation to grow from. I love you even more deeply for your faith in me.

To my beautiful girls, Eva and Honor, thank you for your patience and for allowing your mummy to have it all. You amaze me and make me so proud every day, with your growing independence, understanding of others, and creativity. The legacy I'm building will be yours one day.

To my mum, who has always encouraged me to pursue my dreams and tells me how talented I am even when I feel I'm failing. Thank you for loving the stories of my career and my life along the way. It's been a roller coaster at times and I know I've dragged you places you've not wanted to go: thank you, and I love you.

To Dad, the first entrepreneur I ever knew, who really inspired me to build my businesses. Seeing you set up the family business, Young's Garage, with Mum was the most amazing experience for me, because I learnt how to run a business from a very early age. I observed you managing money and people, and, most importantly, being innovative and opening up new marketing opportunities. You taught me two things: you can never stand still, but must keep moving forward, and you need to surround yourself with a team and a community that care like you do. You can't do great things alone. Thank you; I love you for all the learning and laughter.

Thanks also to my mentors and role models, who have taught me to trust, create systems and be value-led. Special thanks to my first mentor, Michael Humphrey, to Helen and Colin David in my first fashion role, and to all the English Eccentrics team. You were the best! You taught me that a small and niche business can be fun, fulfilling and unique!

To my incredible team, assistants both past and present, thank you so much for your commitment and your enthusiasm: even when it's been a bit chaotic you've been steady and enthusiastic. We've achieved such great things together and having an opportunity to put this all into stories in the book has helped me see what value we can all bring when we work together. Special thanks to my super ex-PA, Ellen, who really had a hell of a job editing the scribbles of my manuscript and put things in order continuously and effortlessly. I am so grateful to Frances, my new PA, and to Shreya for helping with the final hurdle of getting the pictures and final edits in order. We did this together. To Jess, to Amy: you creative, inspiring mums, you are a privilege to work with. To my sister, thanks for being a model for all my new shapes. To Sophie, to Tori, for letting me borrow you from the yoga studio and then for becoming part of my Bespoke tribe just when we needed that extra support, thank you. To Lucky, thank you for helping us achieve that incredible status of finalist for sustainability in the 2017 Lloyds Bank National Business Awards.

I would also like to thank John Doré and Professor Mary Morrell for their passion, their enthusiasm, and their time in taking the trouble to feed back to me on the gaps before the final draft. Also, I am grateful to Michael Berg for his stunning foreword, and to Monica Or for her contribution and praise quote.

Thanks to all my suppliers and to the business owners behind the incredible manufacturers we work with: Paul, Andy, Janny, Ricky, Mac, Karen, Neville and many more. Lastly, to all my clients: you have given me the privilege of creating beautiful designs and seeing them become part of your brand identity; thank you for the journeys and the opportunities – to our continued successful partnership. To all you beautiful brands who bring textile touches to uplift everybody who comes into contact with your clothes, products and people: here's to your stand-out, unique style.

About
the Author

Katie Young Gerald is a London-based author, entrepreneur and speaker in the glamorous, globetrotting world of fashion, food and textile manufacturing, and the founder of Bespoke Textiles, an award-winning consultancy that designs, develops and delivers unique uniforms, luxury clothing and merchandise collections for high-end hospitality and heritage brands, and of her previous company, Katie Young Design Limited.

KATIE YOUNG
FASHION DESIGNER

GET ZAPPAR
ZAP FOR A VIDEO

7.1 – Use the Zappar app to scan the code and watch the video of my interview taken by the Hospital Club on fun facts about me and my work.
https://www.youtube.com/watch?v=W_bRYy4dU5k

Katie has over twenty-five years' experience of co-creating with luxury and middle-market hospitality and heritage brands such as Soho House, the Ivy Collection, the Ace Hotel, the Honourable Society of Middle Temple and the Hospital Club, to name but a few.

She is passionate about creating unique and timeless designs that are bespoke to your brand style, supported by a sustainable and tailored supply chain that saves waste. She draws on her extensive experience of working with luxury heritage and fashion brands such as English Eccentrics, La Petite Salope, Billy Bragg and Britt Lintner, among others.

After spending five years working for the iconic British textile brand English Eccentrics in the 1990s, Katie lived in Hong Kong, where she built up an extensive network of high-end supply partners that have underpinned her global manufacturing expertise to this day. Over the last twenty-five years she has continued to work with and expand her global relationships from her base in London, where she lives with her husband and her two girls, Eva and Honor. Her design studio is based in Brixton.

GET ZAPPAR
ZAP FOR A VIDEO

7.2 – Use the Zappar app to scan the code and watch the video of an introduction to Bespoke Textiles.
https://www.youtube.com/watch?v=-IV5Z9GPNiY

Katie set up her own luxury ladies' wear label, Forever Young, in 2004 in conjunction with London Fashion Week, creating timeless vintage-inspired classic styles that last forever and are beautifully fitted to flatter a multitude of modern shapes.

Her styles and ethos continue to inspire her work and the collections for her world class clients.

You can connect with Katie to find out more about her work and subscribe to her newsletter via her websites to receive interesting updates and hear about future exciting brand collaborations, events and workshops:

- www.katieyounggerald.com
- www.bespoketextiles.co.uk

You can also connect with her on LinkedIn:
- @katieyounggerald

and Instagram:
- @katiegerald, @bespoketextiles

Printed in Great Britain
by Amazon